# THE END TIMES SPIRITUAL WARFARE

Essential Prayers and Sacramentals
For Deliverance and Protection!

Mother and Refuge

**Mother and Refuge Books**

Copyright © 2022 Mother and Refuge of the End Times

No part of this book may be reproduced, or stored in a retrieval system, or transmitted in any form or by any means, electronic, mechanical, photocopying, recording, or otherwise, without express written permission of the publisher.
ISBN: 9798366010337
Cover design by: Ron Ray
Printed in the United States of America
The contents of this book are a combination of prayers from the public domain and content used with the permission of the following:
The Marian Fathers of the Immaculate Conception of the BVM, Stockbridge, MA USA
The Association of the Precious Blood of Jesus (PreciousBloodInternational.com)
Blue Army Press (bluearmy.com)
After the Warning website (AfterTheWarning.com)
The Flame of Love website (flameoflove.us)
Mother and Refuge Website (motherandrefuge.com)

*DEDICATION OF THE BOOK:*
*This book is dedicated to the amazing team of volunteers and workers at 'Mother and Refuge of the End Times.' The voiceover artists, video editors, contributors, designers, writers, hosts, guests and more.*
*It is their faithful dedication that makes this ministry possible.*
*We give thanks to all our supporters and pray for their health, safety and discernment in the times ahead.*

# CONTENTS

Title Page
Copyright
Dedication
PREFACE                                                                 1
INTRODUCTION                                                            2
CHAPTER ONE: SACRED SCRIPTURE FOR DELIVERANCE AND PROTECTION            4
CHAPTER TWO: ST BENEDICT PRAYERS OF EXORCISM AND DELIVERANCE           16
CHAPTER THREE: ST. ANTHONY THE GREAT – DESERT FATHER                   31
CHAPTER FOUR: ST. CHARBEL – LEBANESE HERMIT                            42
CHAPTER FIVE: ST. PADRE PIO                                            58
CHAPTER SIX: ST MICHAEL THE ARCHANGEL & THE HOLY ANGELS – DELIVERANCE PRAYERS   67
CHAPTER SEVEN: ST JOSEPH – TERROR OF                                   87

DEMONS

CHAPTER EIGHT: OUR QUEEN & MOTHER – PRAYERS OF PROTECTION — 93

CHAPTER NINE: MOST PRECIOUS BLOOD DELIVERANCE AND CRUCIFIX PRAYERS AND SACRAMENTALS — 116

CHAPTER TEN: VARIOUS DELIVERANCE PRAYERS OF SAINTS AND EXORCISTS — 126

CONCLUSION: THE PROCESS OF DELIVERANCE: TO BE USED ONLY BY PRIESTS OR EXORCISTS — 151

Acknowledgement — 175

About The Author — 177

Books By This Author — 179

# PREFACE

Dear Readers of the End Times Spiritual Warfare Prayer Book,

This deliverance prayer book is an awakening for all laity to put on the full armour of God in these end times, "so that you can take your stand against the devil's tactics and protect yourselves. "As the Scripture says; "For our struggle is not against flesh and blood, but against the rulers, against the authorities, against the powers of this dark world and against the spiritual forces of evil in the heavenly realms." (Ephesians 6:11-12) Also: "Be calm but vigilant, because your enemy the devil is prowling round like a roaring lion, looking for someone to eat. Stand up to him, strong in faith."(1 Peter 5:8-9)

This prayer book contains the essential powerful deliverance prayers from the Psalms and of the powerful saints that are terrors of demons. Through the intercession of the Immaculate Mother of God and of the Saints, those who pray with it can be delivered from evils and be protected. I bless this prayer book in the "Name of the Father, and of the Son, and of the Holy Spirit." I highly recommend that everyone get a copy. Stay Blessed..

Fr. Dom Francis Mary Kumi (OSB) (Benedictine Monk)

# INTRODUCTION

*BEFORE YOU SAY
THESE PRAYERS*

**Guidelines for Deliverance Prayers for the Laity**

The prayers included in this section are for use by the laity.

The prayers in this section are typically phrased to be used for praying over oneself. All individuals have authority over their own selves and bodies and thus they are free to use both imprecatory prayers (directly commanding demons to leave) and deprecatory prayers (prayers directed to God to cast out the demons).

In the case of praying these prayers for others who are not under their direct authority, we recommend the faithful adjust the prayers so that they are directed to God, thus making it a deprecatory prayer. For their own pastoral protection, we recommend that the faithful not use imprecatory prayers, i.e., directly commanding demons to leave, over others whom they do not have authority.

In accordance with natural law, the laity have authority over their own selves, their spouses and their children. In these cases, they have the authority to use imprecatory prayers.

Source: Catholic Exorcism Website

## *Seeking The Help of the Saints for Protection and Deliverance*

Christians believe what Scriptures clearly teach us (Psalms 141:2, Rev. 5:8, Rev. 8:3-4). That the Saints in Heaven are very much alive in Christ; they are active and are continually praying for Christians and Christ's Church; their prayers rise as incense before God's Heavenly Altar. As a Church, we ask for his protective prayers and intercessions on our behalf.

# CHAPTER ONE: SACRED SCRIPTURE FOR DELIVERANCE AND PROTECTION

## A SONG OF PROTECTION
## PSALM 91

1 He that dwelleth in the aid of the most High, shall abide under the protection of the God of Jacob.

2 He shall say to the Lord: Thou art my protector, and my refuge: my God, in him will I trust.

3 For he hath delivered me from the snare of the hunters: and from the sharp word.

4 He will overshadow thee with his shoulders: and under his wings thou shalt trust.

5 His truth shall compass thee with a shield: thou shalt not be afraid of the terror of the night.

6 Of the arrow that flieth in the day, of the business that walketh about in the dark: of invasion, or of the noonday devil.

7 A thousand shall fall at thy side, and ten thousand at thy right hand: but it shall not come nigh thee.

8 But thou shalt consider with thy eyes: and shalt see the reward of the wicked.

# MOTHER AND REFUGE

## A SONG OF PROTECTION
## PSALM 91

9 Because thou, O Lord, art my hope: thou hast made the most High thy refuge.

10 There shall no evil come to thee: nor shall the scourge come near thy dwelling.

11 For he hath given his angels charge over thee; to keep thee in all thy ways.

12 In their hands they shall bear thee up: lest thou dash thy foot against a stone.

13 Thou shalt walk upon the asp and the basilisk: and thou shalt trample under foot the lion and the dragon.

14 Because he hoped in me I will deliver him: I will protect him because he hath known my name.

15 He shall cry to me, and I will hear him: I am with him in tribulation, I will deliver him, and I will glorify him.

16 I will fill him with length of days; and I will shew him my salvation.

Is there anything that God cannot deliver us and our loved ones from? Are there some things that are just too great for God's deliverance? *Absolutely not!* Please be encouraged as you read these helpful Scriptures, and come to the Throne of grace for God's help, healing, hope... God's deliverance and God's restoration.

## *A Song of Protection – Psalm 91*

Psalm 91 is filled with the goodness and power of God. Great reminders that He faithfully works on behalf of those who love Him.  And at the end of it all, God gives eight reasons why we need not fear.

### Psalm 91's Promises from God

*1. "I will rescue him..."    (deliver, cause to escape)*

*2. "I will protect him..."   (set him on a high place)*

*3. "I will answer him..."   (respond to, speak)*

*4. "I will be with him in trouble..."    (in afflictions, in distress)*

*5. "I will deliver him..."   (rescue, to bring into safety)*

*6. "and honour him..."    (to make rich, strong, heavy with honour)*

*7. "With long life will I satisfy him..." (to have abundance in the journey)*

*8. "and show him My salvation." (let him see My*

*deliverance and victory)*

**During times of pandemic, trial and chastisement, we can call on the Lord for His deliverance. *Psalm 91* is a powerful prayer of protection that we can use to cover ourselves and our families in prayer.**

## *Scripture for Deliverance from Demonic Oppression*

His habitation is above, and the everlasting arms are below. He shall cast out the enemy before your face, and He shall say: 'Be utterly broken!'
Deuteronomy 33:27

Thou art my hiding place; Thou shalt preserve me from trouble; Thou shalt compass me about with songs of deliverance. Selah.
Psalm 32:7

The angel of the LORD encampeth round about them that fear Him, and delivereth them.
Psalm 34:7

For Thou hast been a shelter for me, and a strong tower from the enemy.
~ Psalm 61:3

Deliver me, O my God, out of the hand of the wicked, out of the hand of the unrighteous and cruel man. Psalm 71:4

Behold, the hand of the Lord has not been shortened, so that it cannot save, and His ear has not been blocked, so that it cannot hear.
~ Isaiah 59:1

No object which has been formed to use against you will succeed. And every tongue that resists you in judgment, you shall judge. This is the inheritance of the servants of the Lord, and this is their justice with Me, says the Lord. ~
Isaiah 54:17

For sin should not have dominion over you. For you are not under the law, but under grace.
Romans 6:14

Therefore, confess your sins to one another, and pray for one another, so that you may be saved. For the unremitting prayer of a just person prevails over many things. 1. "I will rescue him..." (deliver, cause to escape)

2. "I will protect him..." (set him on a high place)

3. "I will answer him..." (respond to, speak)

4. "I will be with him in trouble..." (in afflictions,

in distress)

5. "I will deliver him..." (rescue, to bring into safety)

6. "and honour him..." (to make rich, strong, heavy with honour)

7. "With long life will I satisfy him..." (to have abundance in the journey)

8. "and show him My salvation." (let him see My deliverance and victory)

James 5:16

Therefore, be subject to God. But resist the devil, and he will flee from you.
~ James 4:7

Heal me, O Lord, and I will be healed. Save me, and I will be saved. For You are my praise.
~ Jeremiah 17:14

The Lord has freed me from every evil work, and He will accomplish salvation by His Heavenly Kingdom. To Him be glory forever and ever. Amen.
2 Timothy 4:18

For though we walk in the flesh, we do not battle according to the flesh. For the weapons of our battles are not carnal, yet still they are powerful with God, unto the destruction of fortifications: Tearing down every counsel
2 Corinthians 10:3-4

Therefore, let us go forth with confidence toward the Throne of grace, so that we may obtain mercy, and find grace, in a helpful time.
Hebrews 4:16

Source: Catholic Public Domain Bible

## *How to use these Scripture verses:*

Aspirations or ejaculatory prayers are part of the Catholic spiritual tradition. An ejaculatory prayer is a secret and sudden lifting up of the soul's desires to God, upon any emergency that may occur in providence.

One may engage in this prayer by a simple thought darted up to Heaven, or by words from Scripture uttered in the mind, yet so as the voice cannot be heard, as we read that Hannah did, 1 Sam. 1:13.

It helps us to maintain fellowship with God, without any interruption of our lawful callings. It is also a means to repel sudden temptations, and to dispose the heart for a more solemn performance of the stated duties of prayer and praise in the season of them.

Pope John Paul II, in addressing the Psalms, has said that ancient monks used parts of the Psalms as brief prayers "to release a special 'energy' of the Holy Spirit." The Pope added that this use of the Psalms is known as 'ejaculatory prayer' – from the Latin word 'iaculum' that is 'a dart' – to indicate concise phrases from the Psalms which they could 'let fly' almost like flaming arrows, for example, against temptations.

Source: Mother and Refuge Website

## *Psalm 51: Prayer for Cleansing and Pardon*

[1] HAVE MERCY ON ME, O GOD, according to Thy steadfast love;
according to Thy abundant mercy
blot out my transgressions.

[2] Wash me thoroughly from my iniquity,
and cleanse me from my sin!

[3] For I know my transgressions,
and my sin is ever before me.

[4] Against Thee, Thee only, have I sinned,
and done that which is evil in Thy sight,
so that Thou art justified in Thy sentence
and blameless in Thy judgment.

[5] Behold, I was brought forth in iniquity,
and in sin did my mother conceive me.

[6] Behold, Thou desirest truth in the inward being;
therefore teach me wisdom in my secret heart.

[7] Purge me with hyssop, and I shall be clean;
wash me, and I shall be whiter than snow.

[8] Fill me with joy and gladness;
let the bones which Thou hast broken rejoice.

[9] Hide Thy face from my sins,

and blot out all my iniquities.

¹⁰ Create in me a clean heart, O God,
and put a new and right spirit within me.

¹¹ Cast me not away from Thy presence,
and take not Thy Holy Spirit from me.

¹² Restore to me the joy of Thy salvation,
and uphold me with a willing spirit.

¹³ Then I will teach transgressors Thy ways,
and sinners will return to Thee.

¹⁴ Deliver me from bloodguiltiness, O God,
O God of my salvation,
and my tongue will sing aloud of Thy deliverance.

¹⁵ O Lord, open Thou my lips,
and my mouth shall show forth Thy praise.

¹⁶ For Thou hast no delight in sacrifice;
were I to give a burnt offering, Thou
wouldst not be pleased.

¹⁷ The sacrifice acceptable to God is a broken spirit;
a broken and contrite heart, O God,
Thou wilt not despise.

¹⁸ Do good to Zion in Thy good pleasure;
rebuild the walls of Jerusalem,

¹⁹ then wilt Thou delight in right sacrifices,

in burnt offerings and whole burnt offerings; then bulls will be offered on Thy altar. *(Psalm 51)*

# CHAPTER TWO: ST BENEDICT PRAYERS OF EXORCISM AND DELIVERANCE

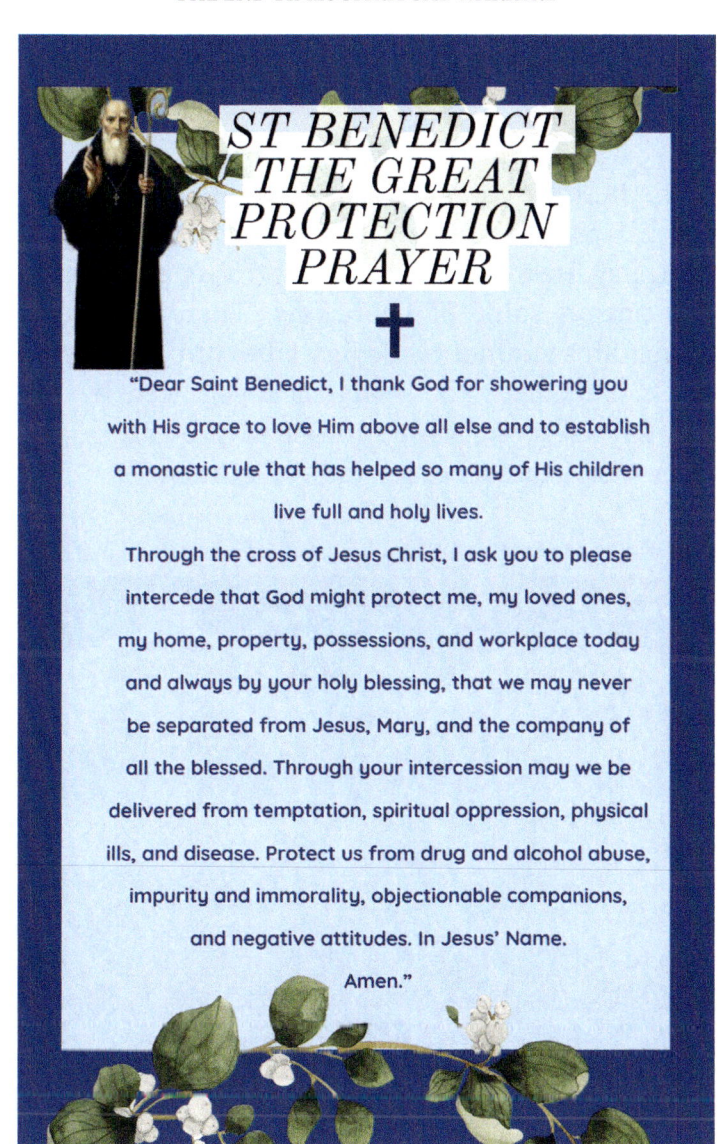

## ST BENEDICT THE GREAT PROTECTION PRAYER

✝

"Dear Saint Benedict, I thank God for showering you with His grace to love Him above all else and to establish a monastic rule that has helped so many of His children live full and holy lives.

Through the cross of Jesus Christ, I ask you to please intercede that God might protect me, my loved ones, my home, property, possessions, and workplace today and always by your holy blessing, that we may never be separated from Jesus, Mary, and the company of all the blessed. Through your intercession may we be delivered from temptation, spiritual oppression, physical ills, and disease. Protect us from drug and alcohol abuse, impurity and immorality, objectionable companions, and negative attitudes. In Jesus' Name.

Amen."

## *The Patron Saint of Exorcisms*

Christians are called to pray to St. Benedict to ask for his protection against evil. He himself led a battle against evil influences and was proclaimed the patron saint of exorcisms. There even is a Christian sacramental dedicated to him: the Medal of St. Benedict. The Medal is recognized by the Church as a powerful symbol of protection and liberation against curses and evil influences.

**Benedict Medal With Exorcism and Blessing (by a priest)**

## *St. Benedict's Medal Prayer*

MAY THE HOLY CROSS BE MY LIGHT,
May the dragon never be my guide
Get away, Satan!
Never tempt me with your vanities!
What you offer me is evil,
Drink the poison yourself! Amen.

**Meaning of the Medal**

The St. Benedict Medal is rich in meaning. The front features an image of St. Benedict holding a cross, the symbol of our salvation, and the monastic patriarch's most powerful weapon. According to St. Gregory the Great who authored his biography, it was by means of the Sign of the Cross that he overcame temptations, shattered a poisoned cup meant to kill him, dispersed the devil's phantom vision of the Monastery of Monte Cassino being set aflame. He prescribed it to his disciples to work countless miracles, including the calming of storms, the freeing of captives, protecting a worker from a fall from the top of a church tower, driving away demons, etc.

His left hand holds his famous monastic rule which exhorts us to "set out on this [God's] way, with the Gospel for our guide."

He is flanked by two pedestals: One carries a poisoned cup which shattered upon his making the Sign of the Cross over it; on the other is perched the raven that took away a poisoned loaf of bread he was offered.

Beneath him are the words, "From the Holy Mount of Cassino, 1880," for this Jubilee Medal was struck to commemorate the birth of the saint 1,400 years earlier.

The outer edge contains the words in Latin, *"May we at our death be fortified by his presence."* St Benedict is a favourite patron for a happy death, for he himself died standing in the chapel at Montecassino, with his arms raised to Heaven, supported by his monks, shortly upon receiving the 'Bread of Angels'.

The back of the medal is even more interesting. It contains a series of initials that stand for a Latin exorcism prayer, as well as a prayer for guidance.

Emblazoned on the prominently placed cross are the letters C S S M L – N D S M D, which stand for the Latin prayer:

*Crux sacra sit mihi lux!*
*Nunquam draco sit mihi dux!*

Translated, it means:

*May the Holy Cross be my light;*
*Let not the dragon be my guide.*

In the four corners of the Cross are the letters C.S.P.B. meaning, *Crux Santi Patris Benedicti* or *"The cross of the holy father, St. Benedict."*

Surrounding the outer rim of the back are the letters V R S N S M V – S M Q L I V B. These letters stand for an exorcism prayer based on an incident from St. Benedict's life.

After St. Benedict had been a hermit for three years, and his reputation for holiness had spread far and wide, he was asked by a group of monks to be their abbot. St. Benedict agreed, but some rebellious monks in the community *really* disliked this idea, and they decided to kill St. Benedict by poisoning his bread and wine. As St. Benedict made the Sign of the Cross over his food, as was his custom, he immediately knew that they had been poisoned. He threw the wine on the ground, saying:

*Vade retro Satana!*
*Nunquam suade mihi vana!*
*Sunt mala quae libas.*
*Ipse venena bibas!*

**This means:**

*Begone, Satan,*
*Do not suggest to me thy vanities!*
*Evil are the things thou offerest,*
*Drink thou thy own poison!*

It is this prayer that is represented by the initials surrounding the back of the medal.

**Use**

St. Benedict medals are used in many ways, but always as a protection against evil. Some people bury them in the foundations of new buildings to keep them free from evil influences, while others attach them to rosaries or hang them on the wall in their homes. But the most common way to use the St. Benedict medal is to wear it. The medal can be worn by itself or embedded in a crucifix.

Regardless of how it is used, the medal should always be blessed using the prayer. While in former times only Benedictines could bless the medal, now any priest can.

Adapted from: Catholic Gentleman Website

## *EXORCISM & BLESSING OF THE MEDAL OF ST. BENEDICT*

**Priest:** Our help is in the Name of the Lord.
*R. Who made Heaven and Earth.*

**P.** IN THE NAME OF GOD THE FATHER † ALMIGHTY, Who made Heaven and Earth, the sea and all that is in them, I exorcise these medals against the power and attacks of the evil one. May all who use these medals devoutly be blessed with health of soul and body. In the Name of the Father † Almighty, of His Son † Jesus Christ Our Lord, and of the Holy † Spirit the Paraclete, and in the love of the same Lord Jesus Christ Who will come on the last day to judge the living and the dead.

*R. Amen.*

**P.** Let us pray. Almighty God, the boundless Source of all good things, we humbly ask that, through the intercession of St. Benedict, Thou pourest out Thy blessings † upon these medals. May those who use them devoutly and earnestly strive to perform good works, be blessed by Thee with health of soul and body, the grace of a holy death, and remission of temporal punishment due to sin. May they also, with the help of Thy merciful love, resist the temptations of the evil one and strive to exercise true charity and justice toward all, so that one day they may appear sinless and holy in Thy sight. This we ask through Christ Our Lord.

**R.** *Amen.*

*The medals are then sprinkled with holy water.*

Source: Roman Catholic Man

## Litany of Saint Benedict

*For Private Use Only.*

LORD, HAVE MERCY ON US, **R.** *Christ, have mercy on us.*
God the Father of Heaven, *R. Have mercy on us.*
God the Son, Redeemer of the world, *etc.*
God, the Holy Spirit,
Holy Trinity, One God,


Holy Mary, *R. Pray for us.*
Holy Mary, Mother of God, *etc.*
Holy Virgin of virgins
Holy Father, Saint Benedict,
Father most reverend,
Father most renowned,
Father most compassionate,
Man of great fortitude,
Man of venerable life,
Man of the most holy conversation,
True servant of God,
Light of devotion,

Light of prayer,
Light of contemplation,
Star of the world,
Best master of an austere life,
Leader of the holy warfare,
Leader and chief of monks,
Master of those who die to the world,
Protector of those who cry to Thee,
Wonderful worker of miracles,

Revealer of the secrets of the human heart,
Master of spiritual discipline,
Companion of the Patriarchs,
Equal of the Prophets,        *R. **Pray for us.***
Follower of the Apostles,
Teacher of Martyrs,
Father of many pontiffs,
Gem of abbots,
Glory of Confessors,
Imitator of anchorites,
Associate of virgins,
Colleague of all the saints,

Lamb of God, Who takest away the sins of the world,
*Spare us, O Lord.*
Lamb of God, Who takest away the sins of the world,
*Graciously hear us, O Lord.*
Lamb of God, Who takes away the sins of the world,
*Have mercy on us.*

V. Intercede for us, O holy father Saint Benedict,
*R. That we may be made worthy of the promises of Christ.*

*Let us pray.*
O God, Who hast called us from the vanity of the world, and Who dost incite us to the reward of a heavenly vocation under the guidance of our holy patriarch and founder, Saint Benedict, inspire and purify our hearts and pour forth on us Thy grace, whereby we may persevere in Thee. Through Jesus Christ, Our Lord. **R. Amen.**

## *Saint Benedict Cross – The Cross of a Happy Death*

The St. Benedict Crucifix (or Happy Death Crucifix) combines two powerful sacramentals, the Crucifix and the medal. The wooden crucifix can be blessed with the Happy Death Indulgence, and the St. Benedict Medal is blessed with powerful exorcisms. It is also the preferred crucifix used by exorcists.

It can be a great aid to those who are in their last agony, when the temptations of Satan are strongest.

What is the *Happy Death Indulgence*?

Whoever at the moment of death, fortified with the Sacraments of the Church, or contrite of heart, in the supposition of being unable to receive them, will kiss this Crucifix and ask pardon of God for his sins, and pardon his neighbour, will gain a PLENARY* INDULGENCE.

(*Plenary*: unconditional, unlimited, unrestricted, absolute; full, complete, entire)

### THE POWER AND EFFECTS OF THE ST. BENEDICT CROSS

The Cross of St. Benedict is very powerful to ward off all dangers of body and soul coming from evil spirits. Saint Benedict used the Cross to dispel evil and exorcise demons. The Cross of St Benedict is still the most used instrument used by exorcists to set the victims of demons free. Missionaries in pagan lands use this Medal with so great effect that it has been given the remarkable name, "The devil-chasing Medal."

The Saint Benedict Cross is a constant reminder for Christians to reject evil temptations, strive to perform good works, exercise true charity and justice toward all. It is a reminder of Jesus calling us to take up our cross and follow Him on the path of love, compassion, and unity. To follow the "true King, Christ Our Lord" and not the lord of culture and convention. To be on the side of justice and bring forth the Kingdom of God. The Medal Cross of St. Benedict must be blessed by a Benedictine Father, or by a priest especially authorised.

The St Benedict Cross is, therefore, a powerful means:

- To destroy witchcraft and all other diabolical influences;
- To keep away the spells of magicians, of wicked and evil-minded persons;
- To impart protection to persons tempted, deluded, or tormented by evil spirits;
- To obtain the conversion of sinners,

especially when they are in danger of death;

- To serve as an armour in temptations against holy purity;
- To destroy the effects of poison;
- To secure a timely and healthy birth for children;
- To afford protection against storms and lightning;
- To serve as an efficacious remedy for bodily afflictions and a means of protection against contagious diseases;
- Finally, the Medal of St. Benedict has often been used with admirable effect even for animals infected with plague or other maladies, and for fields when invaded by harmful insects.

## *Prayer to St. Benedict for a Happy Death*

O HOLY FATHER, ST. BENEDICT, blessed by God both in grace and in name, who, while standing in prayer, with hands raised to Heaven, didst most happily yield thy angelic spirit into the hands of thy Creator, and hast promised zealously to defend against all the snares of the enemy in the last struggle of death, those who shall daily remind thee of thy glorious departure and heavenly joys; protect me, I beseech thee, O glorious Father, this day and every day, by thy holy blessings, that I may never be separated from our dear Lord, from the society of thyself, and of all the blessed. Through the same Christ Our Lord. Amen.

To St. Gertrude, herself a Benedictine nun, St. Benedict revealed that,

> *"whoever reminds me of the extraordinary privilege with which God deigned to glorify my last moments, shall experience my particular assistance in his final combat. I will be a faithful protector against the assaults of the enemy. Fortified by my presence, he will escape the snares of the evil one and safely attain eternal happiness."*

Source: Mother and Refuge Website

# CHAPTER THREE: ST. ANTHONY THE GREAT – DESERT FATHER

## PRAYER FOR SAINT ANTHONY OF EGYPT'S INTERCESSION

O' Glorious Saint Antony, who upon hearing only one word of the Gospel didst forsake the riches and the ease of thy family, thy native land and the world, in order to retire into the wilderness; who, in spite of thy heavy burden of advanced age and the ravages of severe penance, didst not hesitate to leave thy solitude to rebuke openly the impiety of heretics and to restore wavering Christians to a firmer hold upon their faith with all the zeal of a confessor desirous of martyrdom; who through thy conquest of self and the excellence of thy virtues was endowed by Our Lord with miraculous power over animate and inanimate nature; do thou obtain for us the grace to be ever zealous in the cause of Christ and His Church and to persevere even unto death in our imitation of thee, in our belief in revealed truth, and in our keeping of thy commandments and the counsels of the Gospel; to the end that, having faithfully followed in thy footsteps here on earth, we may be enabled to become sharers in thy heavenly glory through all the ages of eternity. Amen.

Our Father, Hail Mary, Glory be three times.

## *PRAYER OF DELIVERANCE BY THE INTERCESSION OF SAINT ANTHONY THE GREAT*

**In the Name of the Father † and of the Son and of the Holy Spirit. Amen.**

O GOD, PHYSICIAN OF THE SOULS AND BODIES that sent Your Beloved Son, Our Lord Jesus Christ, to heal every sick person from all sickness, and to save the human race from the death of sin; you who hurled from Heaven the rebellious demon and all his evil angels to the very depths of hell; You, Lord, heal this creature that belongs to You from all evil of the body and the soul and from all the hold of the devil.

By the grace of Jesus, Your Beloved Son, and by His holy Cross, preserve her from all sickness. Repel evil spirits, so that they have no part or power over her. Crush the devil under Your feet and - through the intercession of the Blessed Virgin Mother of God, the invocation of our father Saint Anthony and all Your saints - free her from all power of invisible and visible enemies, so that she may act according to Your will and give thanks for Your mercy towards her: by the power of Our Lord Jesus Christ, Your only Son, to Whom all glory † and to Your Holy Spirit, for ever and ever. Amen.

O Lord Jesus Christ, Son of the living God, for us men and for our salvation You took flesh of the Virgin Mary, You Who by Your Passion and Your life-giving Death have crushed the gates of hell, bound the victor, and have strengthened us by taking back what he had stolen, repel †, O our God and Saviour, and destroy † all the hold of Satan on Your servant **N.** marked with the Sign † of Your Cross.

Yes, Lord, You Who have driven out the legions of demons and commanded the unclean spirits to come out of the possessed and to depart from them, You Who have said to Your Apostles, "I gave you the power to trample on the serpents and the scorpions and all the opposing powers," protect, O my Lord, Your servant from all evil, from the nocturnal fear, from the arrow that flies during the day, from the walker in the night, and from the noon demon; so that with Your divine help, the prayers of Your Mother, the All-Blessed Virgin Mary, those of our blessed father Saint Anthony and the cohorts of the angelic militia, he (she) may sing Your glory in the faith, the hope and charity, saying,

the Lord is my help, therefore I do not fear what Man can do to me, because You are, Lord, my help, my strength, and my support; that's why I'm not afraid of evil men. For all glory belongs to You, to Your Father, and to Your Holy Spirit, now and forever, and for ever and ever. Amen.

O Holy Spirit Comforter, Who proceeds from the Father and the Son, before Whom we bow down and Who is glorified with the Father and the Son, You Who appeared above the Head of Our Lord Jesus Christ under the appearance of a dove and above the holy Apostles in the guise of tongues of fire, spread out, O Lord, Your strength on Your servant **N.** and drive from him (her) all impure spirits. Dissolve their evil deeds and remove from the body and soul of Your creature the cursed devil, the impure demon, and every kind of evil spirit.

Yes, Lord, we beg You to prevent them from mastering any of his (her) organs, his (her) body, or his (her) soul, and attacking him (her) in no place. By the power of the divine Cross † which is with him (her) and guards him (her) so that he (she) is always and everywhere saved by the intercession of Mary, Mother of God, of our blessed father Saint Anthony and all the saints who glorify You, O Holy Spirit, with the Father † and the Son forever in the ages of ages. Amen.

May the power of the Lord Who reigns over the universe, the Father †, the Son †, and the Holy Spirit † be with him (her), protect him (her), and save him (her) from all defilement of the soul and body, through the intercession of Saint Mary, Mother of God, Saint Anthony and all the saints. Amen.

**V.** May the Lord arise and disperse His enemies!
***R.*** *And let those who hate Him flee from His face!*

**V.** Let them be dispersed like smoke and melt as wax before the fire!
***R.*** *Let the impostors be dispersed before the Lord's Face!*

Glory to the Father †, to the Son and to the Holy Spirit. Amen.

Source: Mother and Refuge Website

## *The Epic Spiritual Warfare of St. Anthony the Great*

The life story of St. Anthony the Great comes from a biography written by St. Athanasius called 'The Life of St Anthony'. It depicts the epic spiritual battles that this 3rd-4th century monk was fighting out in the desert by himself – and what God himself had to say about them.

St. Athanasius says that witnesses visiting St. Anthony at his desert home, *"heard tumults, many voices, and, as it were, the clash of arms. At night, they saw the mountain become full of wild beasts, and him also fighting as though against visible beings, and praying against them."*

St. Anthony experienced many demonic attacks on

his body. The devil *"so cut him with stripes that he lay on the ground speechless from the excessive pain. (He) affirmed that the torture had been so excessive that no blows inflicted by Man could ever have caused him such torment."*

St. Anthony called out, *"Here am I, Anthony; I flee not from your stripes, for even if you inflict more, nothing shall separate me from the love of Christ."*

The demons returned, and St. Athanasius describes what happened next:

> "And the place was on a sudden filled with the forms of lions, bears, leopards, bulls, serpents, asps, scorpions, and wolves, and each of them was moving according to his nature. The lion was roaring, wishing to attack, the bull seeming to toss with its horns, the serpent writhing but unable to approach, and the wolf as it rushed on was restrained; altogether the noises of the apparitions, with their angry raging, were dreadful."

Though he was in terrible pain, St. Anthony responded boldly to the demons:

> "If there had been any power in you, it would have sufficed had one of you come, but since the Lord has made you weak, you attempt to terrify me by numbers: and a proof of your weakness is that you take the shapes of brute beasts.

> "If you are able, and have received power against me, delay not to attack; but if you are unable, why trouble me in vain? For faith in Our Lord is a seal and a wall of safety to us."

Suddenly, the roof opened and a bright light filled the tomb. The demons vanished and his pain ceased. Realizing that God had saved him, he prayed, *"Where were you? Why did you not appear at the beginning to make my pains to cease?"*

And God replied to him: *"Antony, I was here, but I waited to see your fight; since you have endured, and have not been beaten, I will ever be a succour to you, and will make your name known everywhere."*

St. Anthony's spiritual battles continued the rest of his life, until he died at the age of 105.

Adapted from: Church Pop on Mother and Refuge Website

## *Prayer as You Put On Your St. Anthony the Great Medal*

O CHRIST OUR GOD, You taught us the way of true perfection and happiness. You encouraged those who follow You to sell what they have, give to the poor and to take up the cross. When blessed Anthony heard these words, his heart was inflamed with love for You.

He left the world, renounced nation and family and accepted Your easy yoke. He entered monastic life with his companions: mortification, abstinence, and self-denial. By turning away from everything, he turned to You alone; and by dying to himself, he lived for You alone.

For this reason, we honour his memory and say:

Blessed are you, holy Anthony, father of monks and example of religious life; tall cedar on the slope of Mount Lebanon, you have become a prophetic word echoing in the world.

Blessed are you, holy Anthony; you became a lampstand for the Light of the world. By that Light, many have been guided in the way of religious life.

Blessed are you, holy Anthony, morning star in a

world of darkness. Your light made evil fear and caused sin to drawback in fright. How glorious is your Lord, now and forever. Amen.

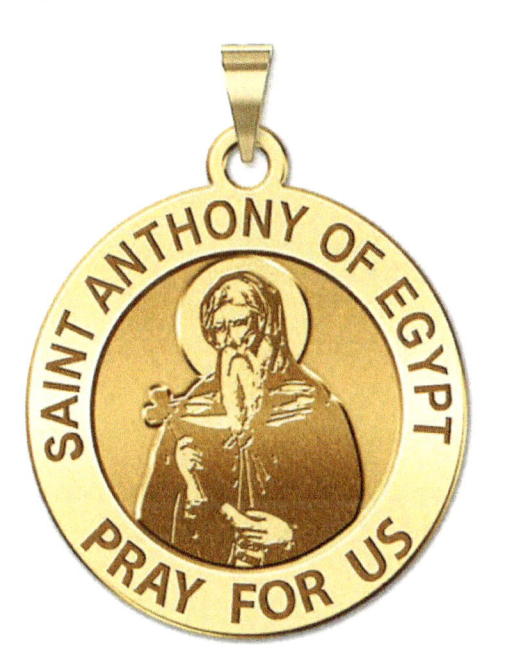

# CHAPTER FOUR: ST. CHARBEL – LEBANESE HERMIT

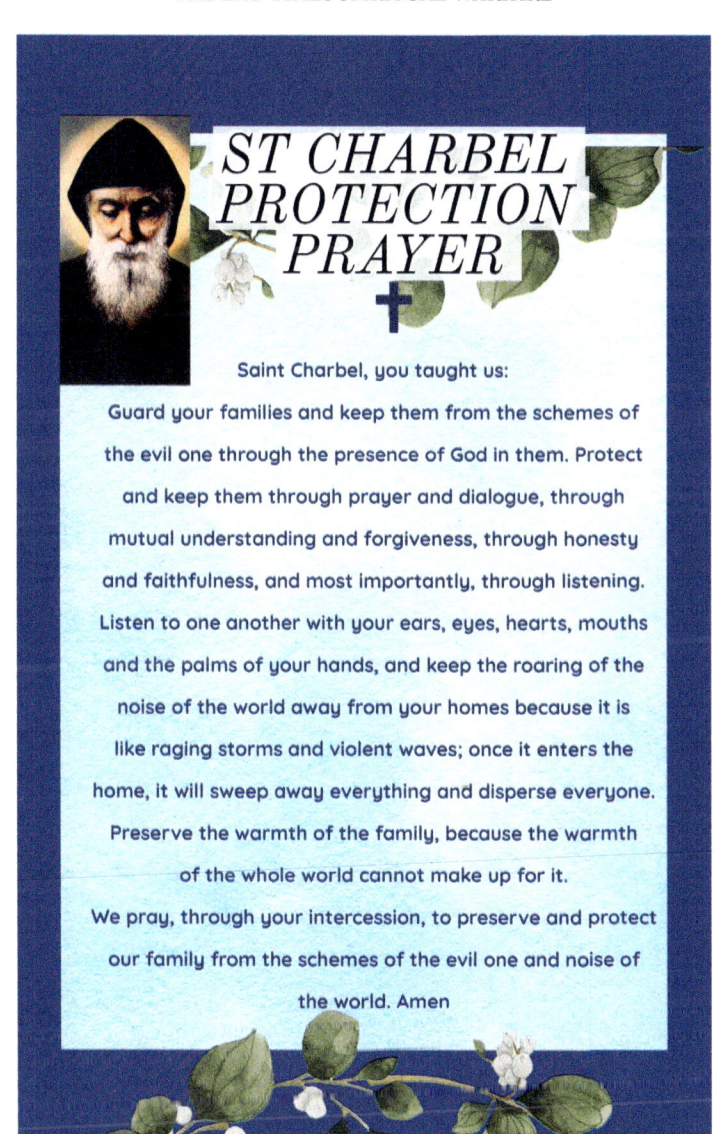

## ST CHARBEL PROTECTION PRAYER

Saint Charbel, you taught us:

Guard your families and keep them from the schemes of the evil one through the presence of God in them. Protect and keep them through prayer and dialogue, through mutual understanding and forgiveness, through honesty and faithfulness, and most importantly, through listening. Listen to one another with your ears, eyes, hearts, mouths and the palms of your hands, and keep the roaring of the noise of the world away from your homes because it is like raging storms and violent waves; once it enters the home, it will sweep away everything and disperse everyone. Preserve the warmth of the family, because the warmth of the whole world cannot make up for it.

We pray, through your intercession, to preserve and protect our family from the schemes of the evil one and noise of the world. Amen

## *Words of St. Charbel Regarding Spiritual Warfare*

*"When Christ ascended, the devil fell. Those people clinging to Him are going with Him, and whoever is standing in His way is subject to falling. Do not hold on to Him and do not stand in His way.*

*"His entire concern is to falsify the image of God in your mind and heart and falsify your own image in your sight. He wants you to know God incorrectly and see yourself wrongly. He falsifies, distorts, and deludes; he tries to magnify you when you should diminish, and diminish you when you should be honoured.*

*"He tries to stop you when you should walk, and make you walk when you should stop, to make you speak when you should be silent, and to silence you when you should speak. He tries to persuade you to hurry when you should slow down, and to walk slowly when you should hasten.*

*"In every case, he wants to mislead you. The devil is the biggest deceiver, the greatest forger, a vicious crook; the Lord and teacher described him as liar and the father of lies.*

*"The devil never comes in his real image, never does he come under an ugly image; he knows what humans like and are attracted to: He tells you about things you like to hear, shows you things you like to see, gives you things you like to touch, and feeds you things you like*

*to taste.*

*"When crooks forge gold, they forge it with something that resembles it: yellow and shining. And so too in order for the devil to fake the image of God – Who is Love in your life – he uses the things that people call love and mixes them up with God, Who is Love. The feelings arising from instinct, passion, the bonds of affection, and the enslaving habits, are all used by the devil to confuse man about the Truth of God, the life-giving love.*

*"The devil's sole concern is to impede those walking up toward the Lord. On your way toward the Lord, the devil wants:*

1. Either to push you off the road: He will create a goal for you that would attract you and toward which you would head, so that you might go astray and be lost.
2. Or he will cause you to fall so you would stop: He will set you a trap in which you would fall.
3. Or he will push you back: He will weary you and discourage you so you would retreat and go back. The important thing to him is that you do not make it.

*"Everything that gathers and unites around good is from God, and everything that divides, and scatters is*

*from the devil. The devil prevails over people through the things of this world; the more Man rids himself of them, the more he is shielded against the evil one, and the more he clings to them, the more he would be under the influence of evil.*

"*The devil is the master of this world. The more you are submerged in the world, the more you come under his power, and the more you detach yourself from the world, the more you free yourself from him. Do not forget that you are not of this world! Do not immerse yourselves in it! Sail through it, rise above it, and raise it to the Lord by the power of Christ elevated on the Cross.*

"*In the beginning the devil makes a man laugh, to make him cry in the end. And he always takes a man to hell while he is laughing, but there, there will be weeping and gnashing of teeth. The man who is now laughing with the devil will surely weep in the end.*

"*God might make you weep in the beginning, but with God you will always laugh in the end. God always makes you weep in order to discipline you, while the devil comes to make you laugh and lead you away from Him, and when God makes you laugh, and the devil comes to make you weep, do not let him fool you.*

"*The devil hates the image of God; he hates the man*

*who is taking on the image of God and wants to distort this image that is in him. The only way Satan can deform the image of God in a person is for him to stop the work of God's Spirit in him. Then, the only image that remains in this person is the image of the animal. The devil's desire is to give to the human being the image of an animal.*

"*The first and essential weapon against the devil is truthfulness; Every word of truth you say is an arrow you shoot into the heart of the evil one. And every honest confession of sin is a spear with which you pierce his heart.*

"*And the next essential weapon is humility. Sincerity and humility mean confession. Confess your sins and you will kill the evil in you.*

"*The devil's only concern is to distract you from God. Beware! He tries to distract you from God even in the matters of God: He distracts you from the meaning of the word that you are praying with the word itself, and he distracts you from praising the Lord, with the melody of the hymn with which you are praising Him. He distracts you from God with the prayer that you are praying to Him.*

"*Remember well that you cannot stand in the face of the devil if you cannot kneel before God. The devil does not come through the windows and apertures that you keep watch over and close well. The devil comes through the door that you open."* (St. Charbel's words to seer Raymond Nadar)

## *Prayer for True Conversion*

O LORD, INFINITELY HOLY AND GLORIFIED IN YOUR SAINTS, You inspired Saint Charbel, the saintly monk, to lead the perfect life of a hermit. We thank You for having granted him the blessing and the strength to detach himself from the world so that the heroism of the monastic virtues of poverty, obedience, and chastity might triumph in his hermitage.

O God, for the blessing of all people You have deigned to choose Saint Charbel as a model of all virtues, and You have converted many souls through his works and example.

We now ask You to grant by his merits and intercession that we may be truly converted, renounce all sins and sinful desire, and become more and more pleasing to You by the practice of true virtue, through Jesus Christ, Our Lord. Amen.

## Hand Print of St Charbel - For the conversion of unbelievers

## *Novena to Saint Charbel*

### Day One

O CHARBEL, SAINT OF GREAT WONDERS, from whose pure and incorruptible body emanates the fragrance of Heaven, come to my assistance and, if it be for the glory of God and the good of my soul, obtain from God for me the grace of which I am in need… *(Name the grace)*. Amen.

Saint Charbel, pray for me.

O Lord, Who granted Saint Charbel the grace of faith, I beseech You through his merits and intercession to grant me that same grace. Then I shall live according to Your commandments and Gospel. To You be glory forever. Amen.

*Our Father, Hail Mary, and Glory Be*

### Day Two

O SAINT CHARBEL, MARTYR OF MONASTIC LIFE who experienced suffering, Our Lord Jesus has made of you a shining beacon. I turn to you and ask through your intercession the grace of… *(Name the grace).* I put my hope in you. Amen.

Saint Charbel, vessel of sweet perfume, pray for me.

O Merciful God, Who honoured Saint Charbel

through the working of great miracles, have mercy on me and grant me what I ask through his intercession. To You be glory forever. Amen.

*Our Father, Hail Mary, and Glory Be*

## Day Three

O BELOVED SAINT CHARBEL, you who shine like a bright star in the firmAmen.t of the Church, be a light for my way and strengthen my hope. From you I ask for the grace of… *(Name the grace).* Ask it for me from the crucified Jesus Whom you unceasingly adored. Amen.

Saint Charbel, model of patience and silence, pray for me.

O my Lord Jesus Christ, Who sanctified Saint Charbel, Your intimate friend, through austerity, mortification, and the carrying of the cross, grant through his intercession that I may bear the difficulties of life with patience and total surrender to Your Divine Will. Then I shall give thanks to You forever. Amen.

*Our Father, Hail Mary, and Glory Be*

## Day Four

O COMPASSIONATE FATHER, SAINT CHARBEL, I turn to you. Confidence in your help fills my heart.

Through the power of your intercession with God, I await the grace for which I ask… *(Name the grace).* Show me once more your power and compassion. Amen.

Saint Charbel, garden of virtues, pray for me.

O my God, Who granted Saint Charbel the grace of imitating You in all virtues, grant that I too, with his help, may grow in the Christian virtues. Have mercy on me. Have pity on me that I may praise You forever. Amen.

*Our Father, Hail Mary, and Glory Be*

## Day Five

O SAINT CHARBEL, BELOVED BY GOD, enlighten me, help me, and teach me to do what pleases Him. Make haste to help me. O compassionate one, I beseech you to ask from God for me this grace… *(Name the grace).* Amen.

Saint Charbel, friend of the Crucified, pray for me.

O my God, I raise my eyes to You. Hear my petition through the intercession of Saint Charbel. Deliver my heart from misery. Grant me peace. Calm my troubled soul. To You be praise forever. Amen.

*Our Father, Hail Mary, and Glory Be*

## Day Six

O SAINT CHARBEL, POWERFUL INTERCESSOR, I ask you to obtain for me the grace of which I am in need... *(Name the grace).*

One single word from you on my behalf suffices to obtain for me the mercy of Jesus, His forgiveness, and an answer to my petition. Amen.

Saint Charbel, joy of Heaven and Earth, pray for me.

O Lord, Who chose Saint Charbel to be our advocate before Your Divine Majesty, grant me this grace through his intercession. Then, with him, I shall glorify You forever. Amen.

*Our Father, Hail Mary, and Glory Be*

## Day Seven

O SAINT CHARBEL, LOVER OF ALL AND HELPER OF THE NEEDY, I firmly hope in your intercession before God. Obtain from Him for me this grace of which I am most in need... *(Name the grace).* Amen.

Saint Charbel, star that guides the straying, pray for me.

O my God, my numerous sins prevent graces from reaching me. Grant me the grace to repent of them. Answer me through the intercession of Saint

Charbel. Bring joy back to my sorrowful heart by granting my petition, O Sea of graces. To You be glory and thanksgiving forever. Amen.

*Our Father, Hail Mary, and Glory Be*

## Day Eight

O SAINT CHARBEL, when in my mind's eye I see you kneeling for prayer, or fasting, or living in austerity, or immersed in conversing intimately with God, my hope and my faith in you increase. Help me, I beg of you, to receive from God the grace for which I am asking… *(Name the grace)*. Amen.

Saint Charbel, inebriated with God, pray for me.

O most sweet Jesus, Who drew towards evangelical perfection Saint Charbel who loved You, I beseech You to grant me the grace to spend the rest of my life according to Your Will. I love you, O God of my salvation. Amen.

*Our Father, Hail Mary, and Glory Be*

## Day Nine

O FATHER, SAINT CHARBEL, here I am at the end of this Novena. My heart is refreshed whenever I speak with you. I have absolute hope that I shall obtain from Jesus the grace which I asked through your intercession. I repent of my sins and promise never to commit them again. I ask you to obtain the fulfilment of my request… *(Name the request).* Amen.

Saint Charbel, crowned with glory, pray for me.

O Lord, Who listened to the prayer of Saint Charbel and granted him the grace of being united with You, have mercy on me in my time of distress and save me from the evils which I cannot bear. To You be glory, praise, and thanksgiving forever. Amen.

*Our Father, Hail Mary, and Glory Be*

Source: Family of St Charbel Website

## *Father of Truth Prayer from Maronite Liturgy of St Charbel*

FATHER OF TRUTH, BEHOLD YOUR SON, a sacrifice pleasing to You. Accept this offering of Him who died for me; behold His Blood shed on Golgotha for my salvation. It pleads for me. For His sake, accept my offering. Many are my sins, but greater is Your mercy. When placed on a scale, Your mercy prevails over the weight of the mountains known only to You. Consider the sin and consider the atonement; the atonement is greater and exceeds the sin. Your beloved Son sustained the nails and the lance because of my sins so in His sufferings You are satisfied, and I live. Amen.

## *Prayer to Obtain Graces*

LORD, INFINITELY HOLY AND GLORIFIED IN YOUR SAINTS, You have inspired Charbel, the saint monk, to lead the perfect life of a hermit. We thank You for granting him the blessing and the strength to detach himself from the world so that the heroism of the monastic virtues of poverty, chastity, and obedience might triumph in his hermitage. We beseech You to grant us the grace of loving and serving You, following his example. Almighty God, Who have manifested the power of Saint Charbel's intercession through his countless miracles and favours, grant us this grace *(here mention your intention)* which we request from You through his intercession. Amen.

Source: Mother and Refuge Website

**Sacramentals known for their power of healing and deliverance - oil, incense, holy water, blessed images and relics from St Charbel's shrine in Annaya Lebanon.**

# CHAPTER FIVE:
# ST. PADRE PIO

# PADRE PIO PROTECTION PRAYER

✝

Padre Pio, faithful servant of God, you know the risks and dangers I face every day. Protect my body, my mind, and my soul from evil snares, and drive away every evil and hateful person present in my daily life. Padre Pio, by the graces granted to you I beg you to intercede for the protection of my home, my family, and my goods, and to take away all material or immaterial threats that could afflict me in any way.

Amen

Padre Pio imitated his Lord Jesus Christ in resisting the devil's cunning temptations, mockery, and persecution both spiritually and physically. From his life, the faithful are enriched with invaluable spiritual warfare lessons for their daily battle with Satan and his minions.

## *Padre Pio's Advice on the Diabolical Battle*

### December 20, 1910

*"I am in the hands of the devil who is trying to snatch me from the arms of Jesus. Dear God! What a war he is waging against me! There are moments in which I am on the point of losing my reason through the continual violence I must do myself. How many tears and groans, dear Father, I send up to Heaven in order to be set free. But no matter, I will never tire of praying to Jesus."*

*Spiritual Warfare Advice*

In writing or speaking to a spiritual director, we can discuss our spiritual struggles and avoid the risk of being isolated. What more we may receive prayers.

We must wilfully make sacrifices of ourselves, and actively engage our free will in resisting temptations of sin. Hence, during our most intense spiritual battles, we must turn to God, not away from Him to be liberated. We must persevere in pray and supplications until the trial ends.

**May 18, 1913**

*"Now, my dear Father, who could tell you all that I had to bear! I have been alone by night and alone by day! From that day I became involved in a bitter strife with those ugly wretches. They tried to make me believe that I had been rejected by God for ever".*

*Spiritual Warfare Advice*

The temptation that God has completely rejected us is a common diabolical tactic. We should cling to the truth of God's covenant of love even in the darkness of spiritual warfare.

We should remain faithful to our obligation to God and keep our eyes fixed on eternal salvation—the bigger context of life.

***June 25, 1911***

*"My dear Father, what is God's purpose in allowing the devil so much freedom? Despair is trying to take hold of me, yet, believe me, Father, I have no intention of displeasing God. I cannot account for and much less understand how it can ever be possible that such a resolute will prepared to do good can be combined with all these human miseries. If you perceive, then, that my soul is in danger, help me, for I want at all costs to*

*save my soul and to offend God no more."*

*Spiritual Warfare Advice*

*During times of spiritual attacks such as temptations and sin, God usually provides someone such as a spiritual director, or confessor, or spiritual friend to help us resist despair or discouragement that are never of God. Despite our human misery, we must continue to be resolute in doing good and seek repentance and confession.*

*We may feel confounded by spiritual attacks but as Pio writes we must want at all costs to save our soul and not to offend God.*

### May 9, 1915

"*The enemies are continually rising up, Father, against the ship of my spirit and they cry out in unison: 'Let us knock him down, let us crush him, since he is weak and cannot hold out much longer.' Alas, my dear Father, who will set me free from those roaring lions all ready to devour me?*"

*Spiritual Warfare Advice*

Though we pass through moments of extreme trial when the crushing power of the enemy is felt and our weakness is all too apparent, trust in God wins the day.

The devil crushes the soul. The Lord lifts the soul. If the Lord reprimands, He does so with gentleness and utmost charity, never crushing the soul. But the devil's aim is soul crushing. Know your enemy. Know yourself. Know the Almighty One. Christ and you proclaim victory over all evil.

## August 4, 1917

*"Satan with his malignant wiles never tires of waging war on me and attacking my little citadel, besieging it on all sides. In a word, Satan is for me like a powerful foe who, when he resolves to capture a fortress is not content to attack one wall or one rampart, but surrounds it entirely, attacks and torments it on every side. My dear Father, the malignant wiles of Satan strike terror into my heart, but from God alone through Jesus Christ I hope for the grace to obtain the victory continually and never to be defeated."*

### *Spiritual Warfare Advice*

In spiritual warfare, by acknowledging our weakness, we depend upon God's mercy. Satan is not interested in half measures against us. Therefore, he attacks from all sides. We must be battle-ready in the state of grace, walking with the Church Militant.

Satan may strike fear in us, but we are able to turn that fear trigger into the virtue of faith because God provides grace.

Adapted from: Catholic Exchange Website

**Image of sculpture depicting St Pio's battles with devils.**

## *St. Padre Pio's Own Prayers to Jesus to Ask for Strength and Protection*

### Padre Pio's Prayers to Jesus for Strength

OH MY JESUS,
give me Your strength when my weak nature rebels against the distress and suffering of this life of exile, and enable me to accept everything with serenity and peace.

With my whole strength I cling to Your merits, Your sufferings, Your expiation, and Your tears, so that I may be able to cooperate with You in the work of salvation.

Give me strength to fly from sin, the only cause of Your agony, Your sweat of Blood, and You Death.

Destroy in me all that displeases You and fill my heart with the fire of Your holy love and all Your sufferings.

Clasp me tenderly, firmly, close to You that I may never leave You alone in Your cruel Passion.

I ask only for a place of rest in Your Heart. Amen.

## St. Padre Pio's Prayer to Jesus for Protection

MAY JESUS COMFORT YOU in all your afflictions.

May He sustain you in dangers, watch over you always with His grace,

and indicate the safe path that leads to eternal salvation.

And may He render you always dearer to His Divine Heart and always more worthy of Paradise. Amen.

## Psalm 37 of David (3-6)

TRUST IN THE LORD AND DO GOOD;

  dwell in the land and enjoy safe pasture.

Take delight in the Lord,

  and He will give you the desires of your heart.

Commit your way to the Lord;

  trust in Him and He will do this:

He will make your righteous reward shine like the dawn,

   your vindication like the noonday sun. Amen.

*Source:* Mother and Refuge Website

# CHAPTER SIX: ST MICHAEL THE ARCHANGEL & THE HOLY ANGELS – DELIVERANCE PRAYERS

## Deliverance Prayer To Saint Michael by Pope Leo XIII

✝

Most glorious Prince of the Heavenly Armies, Saint Michael the Archangel, defend us in "our battle against principalities and powers, against the rulers of this world of darkness, against the spirits of wickedness in the high places"

Come to the assistance of men whom God has created to His likeness and whom He has redeemed at a great price from the tyranny of the devil. Saint Michael Archangel, the Holy Church venerates you as Her guardian, patron and protector; be the glory that you are as Her defender against the toxic terrestrial and infernal powers; God has entrusted to you the souls of the redeemed to place them in the state of their deserved supreme happiness.

Plead to the God of Peace that He crush Satan beneath our feet, so that he may no longer retain men captive nor harm Your Church. Offer our prayers to the Most High so that without any delay the mercies of the Lord may descend on us, and hold captive the dragon, the old serpent, which is the devil and Satan and, once enchained, cast him into the abyss so that he may never again be able to seduce the nations.

Amen.

## Prayer to St. Michael for Exorcism against Satan and the Apostate Angels (favoured by Pope Leo XIII)

O GLORIOUS ARCHANGEL ST. MICHAEL, Prince of the heavenly host, defend us in battle, and in the struggle which is ours against the principalities and powers, against the rulers of this world of darkness, against spirits of evil in high places. Come to the aid of men, whom God created immortal, made in His own image and likeness, and redeemed at a great price from the tyranny of the devil.

Fight this day the battle of the Lord, together with the holy angels, as already thou hast fought the leader of the proud angels, Lucifer, and his apostate host, who were powerless to resist thee, nor was there place for them any longer in Heaven. But that cruel, that ancient serpent, who is called the devil or Satan, who seduces the whole world, was cast into the abyss with all his angels.

Behold, this primeval enemy and slayer of Man has taken courage; transformed into an angel of light, he wanders about with all the multitude of wicked spirits, invading the earth in order to blot out the Name of God and of his Christ, to seize upon, slay and cast into eternal perdition souls destined for the crown of eternal glory. This wicked dragon pours out, as a most impure flood, the venom of his malice on men of depraved mind and corrupt heart, the spirit of lying, of impiety, of blasphemy, and the pestilent breath of impurity, and of every vice and iniquity.

These most crafty enemies have filled and inebriated with gall and bitterness the Church, the spouse of the Immaculate Lamb, and have laid impious hands on her most sacred possessions. In the Holy Place itself, where has been set up the See of the most holy Peter and the Chair of Truth for the light of the world, they have raised the throne of their abominable impiety, with the iniquitous design that when the Pastor has been struck, the sheep may be scattered.

Arise then, O invincible prince, bring help against the attacks of the lost spirits to the people of God, and bring them the victory. The Church venerates thee as protector and patron; in thee holy Church glories as her defence against the malicious powers of this world and of hell; to thee has God entrusted the souls of men to be established in heavenly beatitude.

Oh, pray to the God of peace that He may put Satan under our feet, so far conquered that he may no longer be able to hold men in captivity and harm the Church. Offer our prayers in the sight of the Most High, so that they may quickly conciliate the mercies of the Lord; and beating down the dragon, the ancient serpent, who is the devil and Satan, do thou again make him captive in the abyss, that he may no longer seduce the nations. Amen

## Prayer to St. Michael the Archangel, Commander of the Heavenly Hosts

SO GLORIOUS PRINCE ST. MICHAEL, chief and commander of the heavenly hosts, guardian of souls, vanquisher of rebel spirits, servant in the house of the Divine King and our admirable conductor, you who shine with excellence and superhuman virtue, deliver us from all evil, who turn to you with confidence, and enable us by your gracious protection to serve God more and more faithfully every day. Amen.

## Prayer to St. Michael, St. Gabriel and St. Raphael

MOST HOLY TRINITY, I thank Thee for having formed the hosts of Thy ministers in Heaven so marvellously, and for having adorned their leader so magnificently. Be Thou adored and loved in the beauty and grandeur of Thy ministers: be Thou praised in their jubilant songs of praise and thanksgiving, through all eternity. Amen. O holy princes of Heaven, Michael, Gabriel and Raphael, I praise you for the love with which the Most High has loved you and placed you so near to His own throne. Be mindful of our necessities, and at the head of the Holy Angels, do battle for the Church of God upon earth, that Satan may be forced to yield ever more, and the Kingdom of light and grace, virtue and the holy love of God, may flourish in splendour, and its beauty be acknowledged by all. Amen.

## *Troparion to the Holy Angels from the Byzantine Liturgy*

O LEADERS OF THE HEAVENLY ARMIES, although we are always unworthy, we beseech you that with your prayers you may encircle us with the protection of the wings of your angelic glory. Watch over us as we bow low and earnestly cry out to you: Deliver us from trouble, O princes of the heavenly armies. Amen.

## *To Enoch: Prayer to the Sword of Saint Michael the Archangel*

"After the prayer of the Holy Rosary, pray my Exorcism and the ardent supplication to the Angels, for these are powerful armours to fight the demons and make them flee in disbandment. Remember that you are already in a spiritual battle, and that you cannot lower the guard of your prayer, because the demons roam loose through the world, looking for a way to steal your peace and your soul from you. I give you, brothers, as a present, this prayer to my Sword that you will do morning and night so you remain protected from all the stalking and the incendiary darts of the evil one."

O GLORIOUS SWORD given to Michael the Archangel by the Eternal Father of the celestial realm!

Glorious Sword, fight all spirit of ruin in our families, in our minds and in our hearts.

Glorious Sword of St. Michael the Archangel, place this victorious sign on my right hand to give the final victory and to be able to overcome all of the destructive spirit that wants to lead me away from sanctifying grace.

Come Glorious Sword of St. Michael, flash with a

ray of the Holy Spirit, so that we can see the face of our Heavenly Beloved Father and be worthy of the promises of my Lord Jesus Christ. Amen.

## *Message Regarding Prayer to Guardian Angels for Protection*

"Brothers, pray to your guardian angel, so that he is with you day and night because you are going to need his protection and assistance in the days ahead. There are many guardian angels who are feeling sad because many do not take them into account; remember that we respect your free will, but if you invoke us and ask the Father for our protection, we'll willingly come to serve you.

Pray the prayer of the Guardian Angel morning and night, so that you have their protection and assistance. We Guardian Angels are your friends who watch and intercede for each of you. Do not forget us; remember that we are your protectors and guardians, and we care for each one of you. Our mission is to protect you and lead you down the path that leads to God's Kingdom."

ANGEL OF GOD, my guardian dear to whom God's love entrusts me here, ever this day be at my side to light and guard, to rule and guide. Amen."

## *Chaplet of St. Michael the Archangel*

The Chaplet of St. Michael is a wonderful way to honour this great Archangel along with the other nine Choirs of Angels.

St. Michael promised that whoever would practice this devotion in his honour would have, when approaching Holy Communion, an escort of nine angels chosen from each of the nine Choirs. In addition, for those who would recite the Chaplet daily, he promised his continual assistance and that of all the holy angels during life, and after death deliverance from purgatory for themselves and their relations.

### The Chaplet of St. Michael

O GOD, COME TO MY ASSISTANCE. O Lord, make haste to help me. Glory be to the Father, *etc.*

*Say one Our Father and three Hail Marys after each of the following nine salutations in honour of the nine Choirs of Angels.*

> 1. By the intercession of St. Michael and the celestial Choir of Seraphim, may the Lord make us worthy to burn with the fire of perfect charity. Amen.

2. By the intercession of St. Michael and the celestial Choir of Cherubim, may the Lord grant us the grace to leave the ways of sin and run in the paths of Christian perfection. Amen.

3. By the intercession of St. Michael and the celestial Choir of Thrones, may the Lord infuse into our hearts a true and sincere spirit of humility. Amen.

4. By the intercession of St. Michael and the celestial Choir of Dominations, may the Lord give us grace to govern our senses and overcome any unruly passions. Amen.

5. By the intercession of St. Michael and the celestial Choir of Virtues, may the Lord preserve us from evil and falling into temptation. Amen.

6. By the intercession of St. Michael and the celestial Choir of Powers may the Lord protect our souls against the snares and temptations of the devil. Amen.

7. By the intercession of St. Michael and the celestial Choir of Principalities, may God fill our souls with a true spirit of obedience. Amen.

8. By the intercession of St. Michael and the

celestial Choir of Archangels, may the Lord give us perseverance in faith and in all good works in order that we may attain the glory of Heaven. Amen.

9. By the intercession of St. Michael and the celestial Choir of Angels, may the Lord grant us to be protected by them in this mortal life and conducted in the life to come to Heaven. Amen.

*Say one Our Father in honour of each of the following leading Angels: St. Michael, St. Gabriel, St. Raphael and our Guardian Angel.*

## Concluding prayers:

O glorious prince St. Michael, chief and commander of the heavenly hosts, guardian of souls, vanquisher of rebel spirits, servant in the house of the Divine King and our admirable conductor, you who shine with excellence and superhuman virtue, deliver us from all evil, who turn to you with confidence and enable us by your gracious protection to serve God more and more faithfully every day.

Pray for us, O glorious St. Michael, Prince of the Church of Jesus Christ, that we may be made worthy of His promises.

Almighty and Everlasting God, Who, by a prodigy of goodness and a merciful desire for the salvation of all men, has appointed the most glorious Archangel St. Michael Prince of Your Church, make us worthy, we ask You, to be delivered from all our enemies, that none of them may harass us at the hour of death, but that we may be conducted by him into Your Presence. This we ask through the merits of Jesus Christ Our Lord. Amen.

## Litany to the Holy Angels

LORD, HAVE MERCY. **R. Lord, have mercy.**

Christ, have mercy. **R. Christ, have mercy.**

Lord, have mercy. **R. Lord, have mercy.**

Christ, hear us. **R. Christ, graciously hear us.**

God, the Father of Heaven, **R. Have mercy on us.**

God, the Son, Redeemer of the world, *etc.*

God, the Holy Ghost,

Holy Trinity, One God,

Holy Mary, Queen of Angels, **R. Pray for us.**

Holy Mother of God, *etc.*

Holy Virgin of virgins,

Saint Michael, who was ever the defender of the people of God,

St. Michael, who did drive from Heaven Lucifer and his rebel crew,

St. Michael, who did cast down to Hell the accuser of our brethren,

Saint Gabriel, who did expound to Daniel the heavenly vision,

St. Gabriel, who did foretell to Zachary the birth and ministry of John the Baptist,

St. Gabriel, who did announce to Blessed Mary the Incarnation of the Divine Word,

Saint Raphael, who did lead Tobias safely through his journey to his home again,

St. Raphael, who did deliver Sara from the devil,

St. Raphael, who did restore his sight to Tobias the elder,

### R. Pray for us.

All ye holy Angels, who stand around the high and lofty Throne of God, *etc.*

Who cry to Him continually: Holy, Holy, Holy,

Who dispel the darkness of our minds and give us light,

Who are the messengers of heavenly things to men,

Who have been appointed by God to be our guardians,

Who always behold the Face of our Father Who is in Heaven,

Who rejoice over one sinner doing penance,

Who struck the Sodomites with blindness,

Who led Lot out of the midst of the ungodly,

Who ascended and descended on the ladder of Jacob,

Who delivered the Divine Law to Moses on Mount Sinai,

Who brought good tidings when Christ was born,

Who comforted Him in His agony,

Who sat in white garments at His sepulchre,

Who appeared to the disciples as He went up into Heaven,

Who shall go before Him bearing the standard of the Cross when He comes to Judgment,

Who shall gather the elect at the End of the World,

Who shall separate the wicked from among the just,

Who offer to God the prayers of those who pray,

Who assist us at the hour of death,

Who carried Lazarus into Abraham's bosom,
*R. Pray for us.*


Who conduct to Heaven the souls of the just,

Who perform signs and wonders by the power of God,

Who are sent to minister for those who shall receive the inheritance of salvation,

Who are set over kingdoms and provinces,

Who have often put to flight armies of enemies,

Who have often delivered God's servants from prison and other perils of this life,

Who have often consoled the holy martyrs in their torments,

Who are wont to cherish with peculiar care the prelates and princes of the Church,

All ye holy orders of blessed spirits,

From all dangers, **R. Deliver us, O Lord.**

From the snares of the devil, *etc.*

From all heresy and schism,

From plague, famine and war,

From sudden and unlooked-for death,

From everlasting death,

Through Thy holy Angels, **R. We beseech Thee, hear us.**

That Thou would spare us, *etc.*

That Thou would pardon us, **R. We beseech Thee, hear us.**

That Thou would govern and preserve Thy Holy Church, *etc.*

That Thou would protect our Apostolic Prelate and all ecclesiastical orders,

That Thou would grant peace and security to kings

and all Christian princes,

That Thou would give and preserve the fruits of the earth,

That Thou would grant eternal rest to all the faithful departed,

Lamb of God, Who takes away the sins of the world,

*R. Spare us, O Lord.*

Lamb of God, Who takes away the sins of the world,

*R. Graciously hear us, O Lord.*

Lamb of God, Who takes away the sins of the world,

*R. Have mercy on us.*

Lord, have mercy. *R. Christ, have mercy.*

Lord, have mercy. *R. Christ, have mercy.*

*Our Father..., Hail Mary..., Glory Be...*

V. Bless the Lord, all ye Angels.

*R. Ye who are mighty in strength, who fulfill His commandments, hearkening unto the voice of His words.*

V. He hath given His Angels charge concerning thee,

*R. To keep thee in all thy ways.*

*Let us pray.*

O God, who dost arrange the services of Angels and men in a wonderful order, mercifully grant that our life may be protected on Earth by those who always do Thee service in Heaven, through Jesus Christ Thy Son, Who with Thee and the Holy Ghost are one God now and forever.

O God, Who in Thine unspeakable Providence dost send Thine Angels to keep guard over us, grant unto Thy suppliants that we may be continually defended by their protection and may rejoice eternally in their society, through Jesus Christ Our Lord, Who lives and reigns with Thee, in the unity of the Holy Ghost, forever and ever.

*R. Amen.*

## Scapular of Saint Michael the Archangel

The scapular was given to mystic Marie Julie-Jahenny and was approved by Pope Leo XIII. The enrollment prayer is to be said by a priest:

V. Our help is in the name of the Lord.

R. Who made heaven and earth.

V. The Lord be with you.

R. And with thy spirit.

Let us pray:

O Almighty, everlasting God, Who dost graciously defend thy Church from the wiles of the devil through St. Michael the Archangel, we suppliantly implore thee to bless † and sanctify † this token introduced for arousing and fostering devotion among thy faithful toward this great protector. And do thou grant all who wear it may be strengthened by the same holy archangel, so as to vanquish the enemies of body and soul, both in this life and at the hour of death. Through Christ our Lord.

R. Amen

The priest then sprinkles the scapular with holy water, and then bestows it, saying: Receive brother (sister), the scapular of St. Michael the Archangel, so that by his constant intercession thou mayest be disposed to lead a holy life.

R. Amen.

Let us pray. We appeal to thy goodness, O Lord that thou wouldst hear our prayers and graciously bless † this servant (handmaid) of thine, who has been placed under the special patronage of St. Michael the Archangel. Through his intercession may he (she) avoid and guard against whatever is displeasing to thee, and thus merit in serving thee to accomplish his (her) own sanctification and that of others.

# Scapular of St Michael!

Promises:
1. Exclusive guardianship & protection!
2. Fortify every Christian battle!
3. Vanquish the enemy at the hour of death!

# CHAPTER SEVEN: ST JOSEPH – TERROR OF DEMONS

# Terror of Demons Prayer to St. Joseph

✝

Saint Joseph, Terror of Demons,

cast your solemn gaze upon the devil and all his minions,

and protect us with your mighty staff.

You fled through the night to avoid the devil's wicked designs;

now with the power of God, smite the demons as they flee from you.

Grant special protection, we pray, for children, fathers, families and the dying.

By God's grace, no demon dare approach while you are near.

So, we beg of you, always be near us.

Amen

## Prayer to Saint Joseph, Asking for His Protection

*"Little ones, I give you this prayer of protection so that you may pray it in faith and be strengthened in temptation, so that you can defeat the enemy of your soul."*

O GLORIOUS SAINT JOSEPH! For your deep humility, for your unalterable meekness, for your invincible patience, for your angelic purity and for your perfect fidelity that made you a punctual imitator of the virtues of Jesus and of Mary, I ask you to console me in all my sorrows, to lead me in all my doubts, to defend me in all temptations, to deliver me from all spiritual and material dangers. Extend your arm against all my visible and invisible enemies, by breaking and disrupting all the bonds and the ambushes they lay down and put against me. Amen.

## Litany to St. Joseph

*"After the Virgin Mary, demons fear St. Joseph more than any other saint. The power of St. Joseph is truly extraordinary. He alone bears the title 'Terror of Demons.'"*

As written by Blessed Bartolo Longo, *"Pronounce often and with great confidence the names of Jesus, Mary, and Joseph. Their names bring peace, love, health, blessings, majesty, glory, admiration, joy, happiness, and veneration. Their holy names are a blessing to angels and men, and a terror to demons."*

LORD, HAVE MERCY ON US. *R. Lord, have mercy on us*
Christ, have mercy on us. *R. Christ, have mercy on us*
Lord, have mercy on us. *R. Lord, have mercy on us*
Christ, hear us. *R. Christ, graciously hear us.*

God the Father of Heaven, **R. Have mercy on us.**
God the Son, Redeemer of the world, *etc.*
God, the Holy Spirit,
Holy Trinity, One God,

Holy Mary, **R. Pray for us.**
Saint Joseph, *etc.*
Illustrious Scion of David, Light of Patriarchs,
Spouse of the Mother of God,
Chaste guardian of the Virgin,
Foster-father of the Son of God,
Watchful defender of Christ,
Head of the Holy Family,
Joseph most just,
Joseph most chaste,
Joseph most prudent, **R. pray for us.**
Joseph most valiant, *etc.*
Joseph most obedient,

Joseph most faithful,
Mirror of patience,
Lover of poverty,
Model of workmen,
Example to parents,
Guardian of virgins,
Pillar of families,
Solace of the afflicted,
Hope of the sick,
Patron of the dying,
Terror of demons,
Protector of the Church,

Lamb of God, who takes away the sins of the world, *R. Spare us, O Lord.*
Lamb of God, who takes away the sins of the world, *R. Graciously hear us, O Lord.*
Lamb of God, who takes away the sins of the world, *R. Have mercy on us.*

V. He made him lord over his house,
*R. And the ruler of all his possessions.*

Let us pray.
Lord Jesus Christ, by your ineffable providence you chose saint Joseph to be the spouse of your most holy Mother: grant, we beseech you, that we may have him for an intercessor in heaven, as we venerate him as our protector on earth. You who live and reign forever and ever. *R. Amen.*

## *PRAYER TO SAINT JOSEPH AFTER THE ROSARY/LITANY*

TO YOU, O BLESSED JOSEPH, we come in our trials, and having asked the help of your most holy Spouse, we confidently ask your patronage also. Through that sacred bond of charity which united you to the Immaculate Virgin Mother of God and through the fatherly love with which you embraced the Child Jesus, we humbly beg you to look graciously upon the beloved inheritance which Jesus Christ purchased by His blood, and to aid us in our necessities with your power and strength.

O most provident guardian of the Holy Family, defend the chosen children of Jesus Christ. Most beloved father, dispel the evil of falsehood and sin. Our most mighty protector, graciously assist us from Heaven in our struggle with the powers of darkness. And just as you once saved the Child Jesus from mortal danger, so now defend God's Holy Church from the snares of her enemies and from all adversity. Shield each one of us by your constant protection, so that, supported by your example and your help, we may be able to live a virtuous life, to die a holy death, and to obtain eternal happiness in Heaven.

*R. Amen.*

# CHAPTER EIGHT: OUR QUEEN & MOTHER – PRAYERS OF PROTECTION

## PRAY TO MARY FOR LIBERATION

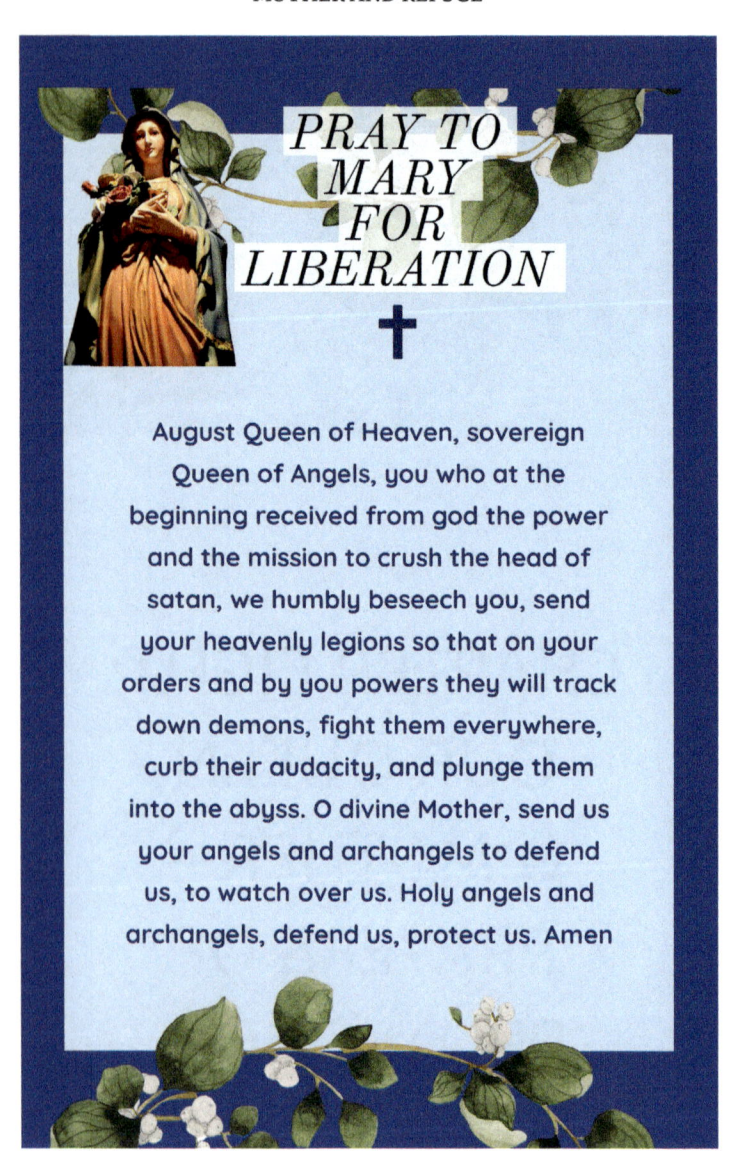

✝

August Queen of Heaven, sovereign Queen of Angels, you who at the beginning received from god the power and the mission to crush the head of satan, we humbly beseech you, send your heavenly legions so that on your orders and by you powers they will track down demons, fight them everywhere, curb their audacity, and plunge them into the abyss. O divine Mother, send us your angels and archangels to defend us, to watch over us. Holy angels and archangels, defend us, protect us. Amen

## *Memorare*

REMEMBER, O MOST GRACIOUS VIRGIN MARY, that never was it known that anyone who fled to Thy protection, implored Thy help, or sought Thy help, was left unaided. Inspired with this confidence, we fly unto Thee, O Virgin of virgins, our Mother; to Thee do we come; before Thee we stand, sinful and sorrowful. O Mother of the Word Incarnate, despise not our petitions, but, in Thy mercy, hear and answer us. Amen.

## *The Power of the Miraculous Medal to Protect and Deliver*

Allow the Miraculous Medal to remind you that you are blessed by the loving protection of our Blessed Mother and preserved in the grace of Her Son. Keep close to them at every moment so you can live and act according to Their teachings and examples.

> Then Mary asked Catherine (now St. Catherine Labouré): "Have a medal struck upon this model of My image. Those who wear it will receive great graces" ... The first medals were made in 1832 and were distributed in Paris. Almost immediately the blessings that Mary had promised began to shower down on those who wore Her medal. The devotion spread like wildfire. Marvels of grace and health, peace and prosperity, followed in its wake. Before long, people were calling it the "Miraculous Medal." In French, the words on the medal say, "O Mary,

conceived without sin, pray for us who have recourse to Thee." It is a great testimony to faith and the power of trusting prayer. Its greatest miracles are those of patience, forgiveness, repentance, and faith. God uses a medal, not as a sacrAmen.t, but as an agent, an instrument in bringing to pass certain marvellous results.

Adapted from **My Saint My Hero**

## *Novena Prayer to Our Lady of the Miraculous Medal*

O IMMACULATE VIRGIN MARY, Mother of Our Lord Jesus and our Mother, penetrated with the most lively confidence in Your all-powerful and never-failing intercession, manifested so often through the Miraculous Medal, we Your loving and trustful children implore You to obtain for us the graces and favours we ask during this Novena, if they be beneficial to our immortal souls, and the souls for whom we pray.

***(Here privately form your petitions.)***

You know, O Mary, how often our souls have been the sanctuaries of Your Son who hates iniquity. Obtain for us, then, a deep hatred of sin and that purity of heart which will attach us to God alone, so that our every thought, word and deed may tend to His greater glory. Obtain for us also a spirit of prayer and self-denial, that we may recover by penance what we have lost by sin and at length attain to that blessed abode where You are the Queen of angels and of men. Amen

## *An Act of Consecration to Our Lady of the Miraculous Medal*

O VIRGIN MOTHER OF GOD, MARY IMMACULATE, we dedicate and consecrate ourselves to You under the title of Our Lady of the Miraculous Medal. May this Medal be for each one of us a sure sign of Your affection for us and a constant reminder of our duties toward You. Ever while wearing it, may we be blessed by Your loving protection and preserved in the grace of Your Son. O most powerful Virgin, Mother of our Saviour, keep us close to You every moment of our lives. Obtain for us, Your children, the grace of a happy death, so that, in union with You, we may enjoy the bliss of Heaven forever. Amen.

MOTHER AND REFUGE

O MARY CONCIEVED WITHOUT SIN, PRAY FOR US WHO HAVE RECOURSE TO THEE

## *Prayer for the Protection of Our Lady of Mount Carmel*

I HUMBLY BESEECH THEE, O LADY OF MOUNT CARMEL, to continue to keep Thy mantle of protection around me and around each of my loved ones. I thank Thee for having done so in the past and for all of your continued help and protection in the future.

### Brown Scapular of Our Lady Our Lady of Mount Carmel

### What is Our Lady's promise in wearing the Brown Scapular?

> "Whoever dies invested with this Scapular shall be preserved from the eternal flames. It is a sign of salvation, a sure safeguard in danger, a pledge of peace and of my special protection until the end of the ages."

### What is the Sabbatine Privilege?

It is the promise piously to be believed, that the Blessed Virgin Mary gave to Pope John XXII in a vision, that She will deliver Her faithful children who have worn the Scapular devoutly from purgatory soon after their death, notably the first Saturday after death.

> "As a tender Mother, I will descend into Purgatory on the Saturday after their death, and will deliver them into the heavenly mansions of life everlasting." (Words of the Blessed Virgin Mary to Pope John XXII).

This Sabbatine Privilege was promulgated and taught through the famous *Bull Sacratissimo Uti Culmine (Sabbatine Bull)* of Pope John XXII in 1322, and given definitive ratification in 1908 by the Holy See.

## What are the requirements for obtaining the Sabbatine Privilege?

1. To wear the Brown Scapular continuously.
2. To observe chastity according to one's state in life.
3. The daily recitation of the Little Office of the Blessed Virgin Mary OR to abstain from meat on Wednesdays and Saturdays OR with the permission of a priest, say five decades of the Holy Rosary.

## *Our Lady Undoer of Knots Novena*

1. Make the Sign of the Cross.

2. Say the Act of Contrition. Ask pardon for your sins and make a firm promise not to commit them again.

Oh my God, I am heartily sorry for having offended Thee. I detest all my sins because I dread the loss of Heaven and the pains of Hell. But most of all, because they offend Thee, my God, Who art all good and deserving of all my love. I firmly resolve, with the help of Thy grace, to confess my sins, to do penance, and to Amend my life. Amen.

3. Say the first three decades of the Rosary.

4. Make the meditation of the day (*see below*).

5. Say the last two decades of the Rosary.

6. Finish with the Prayer to Our Lady, Undoer of Knots

## Meditation for Day 1

DEAREST HOLY MOTHER, MOST HOLY MARY, You undo the knots that suffocate Your children; extend Your merciful hands to me. I entrust to You today this knot....and all the negative consequences that it provokes in my life. I give You this knot that torments me and makes me unhappy and so impedes me from uniting myself to You and Your Son Jesus, my Saviour.

I run to You, Mary, Undoer of Knots because I trust You and I know that You never despise a sinning child who comes to ask You for help. I believe that You can undo this knot because Jesus grants You everything. I believe that You want to undo this knot because You are my Mother. I believe that You will do this because You love me with eternal love.

Thank you, dear Mother.
Mary, Undoer of Knots, pray for me.
*The one who seeks grace, finds it in Mary's hands.*

## Meditation for Day 2

MARY, BELOVED MOTHER, CHANNEL OF ALL GRACE, I return to You today my heart, recognising that I am a sinner in need of Your help. Many times, I lose the graces You grant me because of my sins of egoism, pride, rancour and my lack of generosity and humility. I turn to You today, Mary, Undoer of Knots, for You to ask Your Son Jesus to grant me a pure, divested, humble and trusting heart. I will live today practicing these virtues and offering You this as a sign of my love for You. I entrust into Your hands this knot (...describe) which keeps me from reflecting the glory of God.

Mary, Undoer of Knots, pray for me.
*Mary offered all the moments of Her day to God.*

## Meditation for Day 3

MEDITATING MOTHER, QUEEN OF HEAVEN, in Whose hands the treasures of the King are found, turn Your merciful eyes upon me today. I entrust into Your holy hands this knot in my life...and all the rancour and resentment it has caused in me. I ask Your forgiveness, God the Father, for my sin. Help me now to forgive all the persons who consciously or unconsciously provoked this knot. Give me, also, the grace to forgive me for having provoked this knot. Only in this way can You undo it. Before You, dearest Mother, and in the Name of Your Son Jesus, my Saviour, Who has suffered so many offenses, having been granted forgiveness,

I now forgive these persons...and myself, forever. Thank you, Mary, Undoer of Knots for undoing the knot of rancour in my heart and the knot which I now present to You.

Mary, Undoer of Knots, pray for me.
*Turn to Mary, you who desire grace.*

## Meditation for Day 4

Dearest Holy Mother, You are generous with all who seek You; have mercy on me. I entrust into Your hands this knot which robs the peace of my heart, paralyses my soul and keeps me from going to my Lord and serving Him with my life.

Undo this knot in my love...., O Mother, and ask Jesus to heal my paralytic faith which gets downhearted with the stones on the road. Along with You, dearest Mother, may I see these stones as friends. Not murmuring against them anymore but giving endless thanks for them, may I smile trustingly in Your power.

Mary, Undoer of Knots, pray for me.
*Mary is the Sun and no one is deprived of Her warmth.*

## Meditation for Day 5

MOTHER, UNDOER OF KNOTS, so generous and compassionate, I come to You today to once again entrust this knot...in my life to You and to ask the divine wisdom to undo, under the light of the Holy Spirit, this snarl of problems. No one ever saw You angry; to the contrary, Your words were so charged with sweetness that the Holy Spirit was manifested on Your lips. Take away from me the bitterness, anger and hatred which this knot has caused me. Give me, o dearest Mother, some of the sweetness and wisdom that is all silently reflected in Your heart. And just as You were present at Pentecost, ask Jesus to send me a new presence of the Holy Spirit at this moment in my life. Holy Spirit, come upon me!

Mary, Undoer of Knots, pray for me.
*Mary, with God, is powerful.*

## Meditation for Day 6

QUEEN OF MERCY, I entrust to You this knot in my life...and I ask You to give me a heart that is patient until You undo it. Teach me to persevere in the Living Word of Jesus, in the Eucharist, the Sacrament of Confession; stay with me and prepare my heart to celebrate with the angels the grace that will be granted to me. Amen! Alleluia!

Mary, Undoer of Knots, pray for me.
*You are beautiful, Mary, and there is no stain of sin in You.*

## Meditation for Day 7

MOTHER MOST PURE, I come to You today to beg You to undo this knot in my life...and free me from the snares of evil. God has granted You great power over all the demons. I renounce all of them today, every connection I have had with them and I proclaim Jesus as my one and only Lord and Saviour. Mary, Undoer of Knots, crush the evil one's head and destroy the traps he has set for me by this knot. Thank you, dearest Mother. Most Precious Blood of Jesus, free me!

Mary, Undoer of Knots, pray for me.
*You are the glory of Jerusalem, the joy of our people.*

## Meditation for Day 8

VIRGIN MOTHER OF GOD, overflowing with mercy, have mercy on Your child and undo this knot...in my life. I need Your visit to my life, like You visited Elizabeth. Bring me Jesus, bring me the Holy Spirit. Teach me to practice the virtues of courage, joyfulness, humility, and faith, and, like Elizabeth, to be filled with the Holy Spirit. Make me joyfully rest on Your bosom, Mary. I consecrate You as my Mother, Queen and Friend. I give You my heart and everything I have (my home and family, my material and spiritual goods.) I am Yours forever. Put Your Heart in me so that I can do everything Jesus tells me.

Mary, Undoer of Knots, pray for me.
*Let us go, therefore, full of trust, to the Throne of grace.*

## Meditation for Day 9

MOST HOLY MARY, OUR ADVOCATE, UNDOER OF KNOTS, I come today to thank You for undoing this knot in my life...You know very well the suffering it has caused me. Thank you for coming, Mother, with Your long fingers of mercy to dry the tears in my eyes; You receive me in Your arms and make it possible for me to receive once again the divine grace.

Mary, Undoer of Knots, dearest Mother, I thank You for undoing the knots in my life. Wrap me in Your mantle of love, keep me under Your protection, enlighten me with Your peace! Amen.

Mary, Undoer of Knots, pray for me.

## PRAYER TO MARY, UNDOER OF KNOTS (Closing Prayer For Each Day of the Novena)

VIRGIN MARY, MOTHER OF FAIR LOVE, Mother Who never refuses to come to the aid of a child in need, Mother Whose hands never cease to serve Your beloved children because they are moved by the divine love and immense mercy that exists in Your heart, cast Your compassionate eyes upon me and see the snarl of knots that exist in my life.

You know very well how desperate I am, my pain and how I am bound by these knots.

Mary, Mother to Whom God entrusted the undoing of the knots in the lives of His children, I entrust into Your hands the ribbon of my life.

No one, not even the evil one himself, can take it away from Your precious care. In Your hands, there is no knot that cannot be undone.
Powerful Mother, by Your grace and intercessory power with Your Son and My Liberator, Jesus, take into Your hands today this knot... I beg You to undo it for the glory of God, once for all, You are my hope.

O my Lady, You are the only consolation God gives me, the fortification of my feeble strength, the enrichment of my destitution and with Christ the freedom from my chains.

Hear my plea.
Keep me, guide me, protect me, O Safe Refuge!

Mary, Undoer of Knots, pray for me

## *Litany of the Blessed Virgin Mary (Litany of Loreto)*

The Litany of The Blessed Virgin Mary, also known as the Litany of Loreto, is a popular prayer of supplication, once prayed in processions to atone for sins and to prevent calamities.

Pilgrims at the famous Marian Shrine in Loreto, Italy used it in the 16$^{th}$ century, and it was approved in 1587 by Pope Sixtus V. Although it is often prayed privately, especially after the Rosary, the Litany of the Blessed Virgin Mary has the distinction of being one of only six litanies approved for public recitation by the Holy See.

Its invocations to our Blessed Mother include titles given to Her by the early Church Fathers in the first few centuries of Christianity. The Litany of the Blessed Virgin Mary has also been set to music (as the Litany of Loreto) by such celebrated composers as Palestrina, Charpentier, and Mozart.

LORD, HAVE MERCY ON US.        R.
*Christ, have mercy on us.*

Lord, have mercy on us. Christ hear us.
R. *Christ, graciously hear us.*

God, the Father of Heaven,      **R. *Have mercy on***

*us.*

God, the Son, Redeemer of the world, *etc.*

God, the Holy Ghost,

Holy Trinity, One God,

Holy Mary, **R. pray for us.**

Holy Mother of God, *etc.*

Holy Virgin of virgins,

Mother of Christ,

Mother of divine grace,

Mother most pure,

Mother most chaste, **R. pray for us.**

Mother inviolate,

Mother undefiled,

Mother most amiable,

Mother most admirable,

Mother of good counsel,

Mother of our Creator,

Mother of our Saviour,

Virgin most prudent,

Virgin most venerable,

Virgin most renowned,

Virgin most powerful,

Virgin most merciful,

Virgin most faithful,

Mirror of justice,

Seat of wisdom,

Cause of our joy,

Spiritual vessel,

Vessel of honour,

Singular vessel of devotion,

Mystical rose,

Tower of David,

Tower of ivory,

House of gold,

Ark of the covenant,     ***R. pray for us.***

Gate of Heaven,

Morning star,

Health of the sick,

Refuge of sinners,

Comforter of the afflicted,

Help of Christians,

Queen of angels,

Queen of patriarchs,

Queen of prophets,

Queen of apostles,

Queen of martyrs,

Queen of confessors,

Queen of virgins,

Queen of all saints,

Queen conceived without original sin,

Queen assumed into Heaven,

Queen of the most holy Rosary,

Queen of peace,

Lamb of God, Who takest away the sins of the world,

*R. Spare us, O Lord.*

Lamb of God, Who takest away the sins of the world,

*R. Graciously hear us, O Lord.*

Lamb of God, Who takest away the sins of the world,

*R. Have mercy on us.*

V. Pray for us, O holy Mother of God.

*R. That we may be made worthy of the promises of Christ.*

Let us pray.

Grant, O Lord God, we beseech Thee, that we Thy servants may rejoice in continual health of mind and body; and, through the glorious intercession of Blessed Mary ever Virgin, may be freed from present sorrow, and enjoy eternal gladness. Through Christ Our Lord. Amen.

## Consecration of One's Exterior Goods to the Blessed Virgin Mary

Consecrating of one's exterior goods to the Blessed Virgin Mary is a prayer that is very helpful in blocking diabolic oppression.

I, *(NAME)*, A FAITHLESS SINNER, renew and ratify today in Thy hands the vows of my Baptism. I renounce forever Satan, his pomps and works; and I give myself entirely to Jesus Christ, the Incarnate Wisdom, to carry my cross after Him all the days of my life, and to be more faithful to Him than I have ever been before.

In the presence of all the heavenly court, I choose Thee, O Mary, this day for my Mother and Mistress. Knowing that I have received rights over all my exterior goods by the promulgation of the Natural Law by the Divine Author, I deliver and consecrate to Thee, as Thy slave, all of my exterior goods, past, present and future. I relinquish into Thy hands, my Heavenly Mother, all rights over my exterior goods, including my health, finances, relationships, possessions, property, my job and my earthly success and I retain for myself no right of disposing the goods that come to me but leave to Thee the entire and full right of disposing of all that belongs to me, without exception, according to Thy good pleasure, for the greater glory of God in time and in eternity. As I now interiorly relinquish what belongs to me exteriorly into Thy hands, I entrust to Thee the protection of those exterior goods against the evil one, so that, knowing that they now belong to Thee, he cannot touch them.

Receive, O good and pious Virgin, this little offering of what little is, in honour of, and in union with, that subjection which the Eternal Wisdom deigned to have to Thy maternity; in homage to the power which both of You have over this poor sinner, and in thanksgiving for the privileges with which the Holy Trinity has favoured Thee.

Trusting in the providential care of God the Father and Thy maternal care, I have full confidence that Thou wilst take care of me as to the necessities of this life and will not leave me forsaken.

God the Father, increase my trust in Thy Son's Mother; Our Lady of Fair Love, give me perfect confidence in the providence of Thy Son.

# CHAPTER NINE: MOST PRECIOUS BLOOD DELIVERANCE AND CRUCIFIX PRAYERS AND SACRAMENTALS

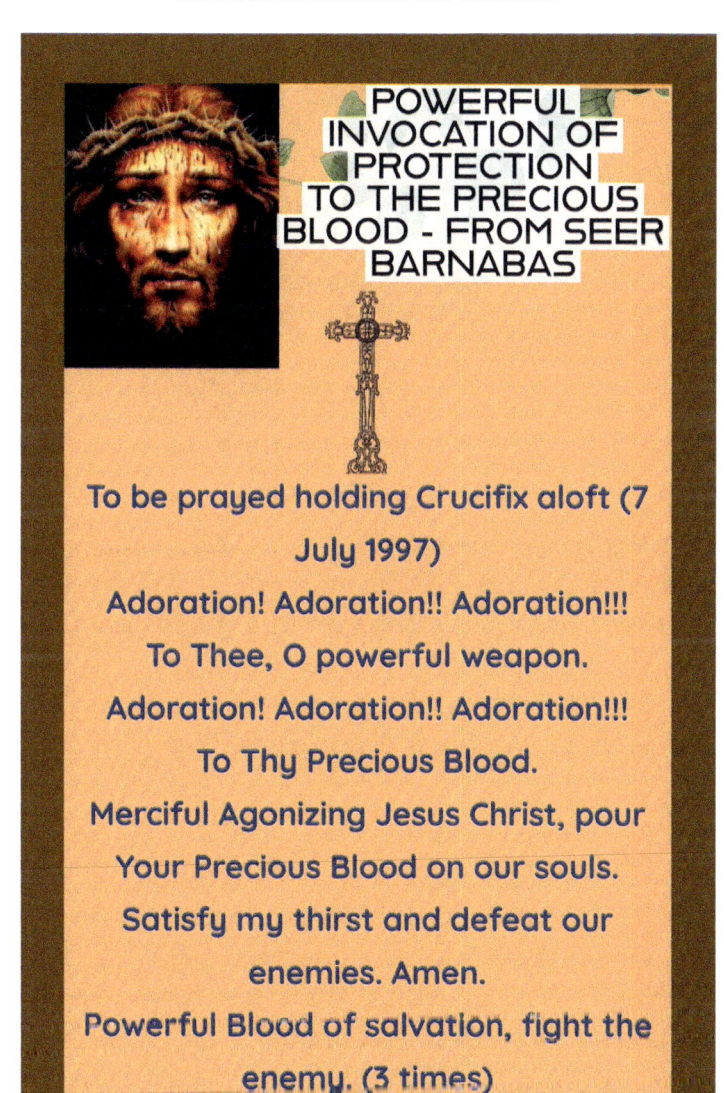

## POWERFUL INVOCATION OF PROTECTION TO THE PRECIOUS BLOOD - FROM SEER BARNABAS

To be prayed holding Crucifix aloft (7 July 1997)

Adoration! Adoration!! Adoration!!!
To Thee, O powerful weapon.
Adoration! Adoration!! Adoration!!!
To Thy Precious Blood.
Merciful Agonizing Jesus Christ, pour Your Precious Blood on our souls. Satisfy my thirst and defeat our enemies. Amen.
Powerful Blood of salvation, fight the enemy. (3 times)

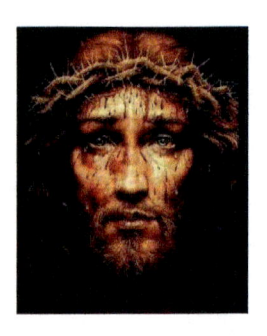

## *CONSECRATION TO THE PRECIOUS BLOOD OF JESUS CHRIST*

CONSCIOUS, MERCIFUL SAVIOUR, of my nothingness and of Thy sublimity, I cast myself at Thy feet and thank Thee for the many proofs of Thy grace shown unto me, Thy ungrateful creature. I thank Thee especially for delivering me by Thy Precious Blood from the destructive power of Satan.

In the presence of my dear Mother Mary, my guardian angel, my patron saint, and of the whole company of Heaven, I dedicate myself voluntarily with a sincere heart, O dearest Jesus, to Thy Precious Blood, by which Thou hast redeemed the world from sin, death and hell.

I promise Thee, with the help of Thy grace and to the utmost of my strength, to stir up and foster devotion to Thy Precious Blood, the price of our redemption, so that Thy adorable Blood may be honoured and glorified by all. In this way, I wish to make reparation for my disloyalty towards Thy Precious Blood of love, and to make satisfaction to Thee for the many profanations which men commit against that precious price of their salvation. O would that my own sins, my coldness, and all the acts of disrespect I have ever committed against Thee, O Holy Precious Blood, could be undone.

Behold, O dearest Jesus, I offer to Thee the love, honour and adoration, which Thy most Holy Mother, Thy faithful disciples and all the saints have offered to Thy Precious Blood. I ask Thee to forget my earlier faithlessness and coldness, and to forgive all who offend Thee.

Sprinkle me, O Divine Saviour, and all men with Thy Precious Blood, so that we, O Crucified Love, may love Thee from now on with all our hearts, and worthily honour the price of our salvation. Amen.

We fly to Thy patronage, O holy Mother of God; despise not our petitions in our necessities, but deliver us always from all dangers, O glorious and blessed Virgin. Amen.

*For All Benefactors of this Devotion*
Our Father*...Hail Mary*. Glory Be*...

## *Prayer of Deliverance: The Most Precious Blood of Jesus*

THROUGH THE BLOOD OF JESUS we find our healing and our deliverance!

We need to be guarded under the Blood of Our Lord Jesus Christ. So I invite you to pray this prayer, that will certainly be a source of healing and deliverance.

*"But for you the blood will mark the houses where you are. Seeing the blood, I will pass over you; thereby, when I strike the land of Egypt, no destructive blow will come upon you."* (Exodus 12.13 NABRE)

And the word of God **confirms**:

For if the blood of goats and bulls and the sprinkling of a heifer's ashes can sanctify those who are defiled so that their flesh is cleansed, how much more will the Blood of Christ, Who through the eternal spirit offered Himself unblemished to God, cleanse our consciences from dead works to worship the living God. (Hb 9.13-14)

Lord Jesus Christ, in Your name, and with the power of Thy Precious Blood, we seal each person, fact or event through which the enemy wants to harm us.

With the power of the Blood of Jesus, we seal all destructive power in the air, on land, on water, on fire, beneath the ground, in the depths of hell and the world in which we move.

With the power of the Blood of Jesus, we break down all interference and evil action. We ask You, Lord, that You send to our homes and workplaces the Blessed Virgin Mary, accompanied by St. Michael, St. Gabriel, St. Raphael and Your entire court of Holy Angels.

With the power of the Blood of Jesus, we seal our house, all who inhabit *(name each one)*, the people the Lord will send, as well as all food and goods that He generously grants us for our livelihood.

With the power of the Blood of Jesus, we seal land, doors, windows, objects, walls and floors and the air we breathe; in faith, we put a circle of Your Blood around our family.

With the power of the Blood of Jesus, we seal places where we'll be this day and people, companies and institutions with whom we will interact.

With the power of the Blood of Jesus, we seal our material and spiritual work, our family business, the vehicles, the roads, the air, the streets and any means of transport that we will use.

With Your most Precious Blood, we seal the acts, the minds and hearts of our country so that Your peace and Your Heart in the end may it reign.

We thank Thee Lord, for Thy most Precious Blood, by which we are saved and preserved from evil.

## Litany of the Most Precious Blood

Christ have mercy. *R. Lord have mercy.*

Christ hear us. *R. Christ graciously hear us.*

God the Father of Heaven, **R. have mercy on us.**

God the Son, Redeemer of the world, *etc.*

God the Holy Spirit,

Holy Trinity, One God,

Blood of Christ, only begotten Son of the Eternal Father, **R. save us.**

Blood of Christ, Incarnate Word of God, *etc.*

Blood of Christ, of the New and Eternal TestAmen.t,

Blood of Christ, falling upon the Earth in the Agony,

Blood of Christ, shed profusely in the Scourging,

Blood of Christ, flowing forth in the Crowning with Thorns,
**R. save us.**

Blood of Christ, poured out on the Cross, *etc.*

Blood of Christ, price of our salvation,

Blood of Christ, without which there is no forgiveness,

Blood of Christ, Eucharistic drink and refreshment of souls,

Blood of Christ, stream of mercy,

Blood of Christ, victor over demons,

Blood of Christ, courage of Martyrs,

Blood of Christ, strength of Confessors,

Blood of Christ, bringing forth Virgins,

Blood of Christ, help of those in peril,

Blood of Christ, relief of the burdened,

Blood of Christ, solace in sorrow,

Blood of Christ, hope of the penitent,

Blood of Christ, consolation of the dying,

Blood of Christ, peace and tenderness of hearts,

Blood of Christ, pledge of eternal life,

Blood of Christ, freeing souls from purgatory,

Blood of Christ, most worthy of all glory and honor,

Lamb of God, Who takest away the sins of the world, *R. Spare us, O Lord.*

Lamb of God, Who takest away the sins of the world, *R. Graciously hear us, O Lord.*

Lamb of God, Who takest away the sins of the

world,       *R. Have mercy on us.*

V. Thou hast redeemed us with Thy Blood, O Lord.

R. And made of us a kingdom for our God.

**Let us pray.**

Almighty, and everlasting God, Who hast appointed Thine only-begotten Son to be the Redeemer of the world, and hast been pleased to be reconciled unto us by His Blood, grant us, we beseech Thee, so to venerate with solemn worship the price of our salvation, that the power thereof may here on Earth keep us from all things hurtful, and the fruit of the same may gladden us forever hereafter in Heaven. Through the same Christ Our Lord.

*R. Amen.*

THE END TIMES SPIRITUAL WARFARE

# CHAPTER TEN: VARIOUS DELIVERANCE PRAYERS OF SAINTS AND EXORCISTS

# A Prayer of Exorcism Taught By Saint Anthony of Padua

✝

In the original Latin, the prayer says

Ecce Crucem Domini!

Fugite partes adversae!

Vicit Leo de tribu Juda,

Radix David! Alleluia!

And translated, it reads:

Behold, the Cross of the Lord!

Begone, all evil powers!

The Lion of the tribe of Judah,

The Root of David, has conquered!

Alleluia, Alleluia!

This short prayer has the flavor of a small exorcism. We can use it too — both in Latin and in English — to be able to overcome all the temptations we face.

## *Prayers Against the Demons of the Seven Deadly Sins*

**Against the Demon of Pride**

O LORD JESUS CHRIST, Pattern of humility, who didst empty Thyself of Thy glory, and take upon Thee the form of a servant: Root out of us all pride and conceit of heart, that, owing ourselves miserable and guilty sinners, we may willingly bear contempt and reproaches for Thy sake, and, glorying in nothing but Thee, may esteem ourselves lowly in Thy sight. Not unto us, O Lord, but to Thy Name be the praise, for Thy loving mercy and for Thy truth's sake. Amen.

**Against the Demon of Covetousness**

O LORD JESUS CHRIST, Who though Thou wast rich yet for our sakes didst become poor, grant that all over-eagerness and covetousness of earthly goods may die in us, and the desire of heavenly things may live and grow in us: Keep us from all idle and vain expenditures, that we may always have to give to him that needeth, and that giving not grudgingly nor of necessity, but cheerfully, we may be loved of Thee, and be made through Thy merits partakers of the riches of Thy heavenly treasure. Amen.

### Against the Demon of Lust

O LORD JESUS CHRIST, Guardian of chaste souls, and Lover of purity, Who wast pleased to take our nature and to be born of an immaculate Virgin: Mercifully look upon my infirmity. Create in me a clean heart, O God, and renew a right spirit within me; help me to drive away all evil thoughts, to conquer every sinful desire, and so pierce my flesh with the fear of Thee that, this worst enemy being overcome, I may serve Thee with a chaste body and please Thee with a pure heart. Amen.

### Against the Demon of Anger

O MOST MEEK JESUS, Prince of Peace, Who when Thou wast reviled, didst not revile, and on the Cross didst pray for Thy murderers: Implant in our hearts the virtues of gentleness and patience, that, restraining the fierceness of anger, impatience, and resentment, we may overcome evil with good, for Thy sake love our enemies, and as children of our Heavenly Father seek Thy peace and evermore rejoice in Thy love. Amen.

### Against the Demon of Gluttony

O LORD JESUS CHRIST, Mirror of abstinence, Who, to teach us the virtue of abstinence, didst fast forty days and forty nights, grant that, serving Thee and not our own appetites, we may live soberly and piously with contentment, without greediness, gluttony, or drunkenness, that Thy Will being our meat and drink, we may hunger and thirst after justice, and finally obtain from Thee that Food which endureth unto life eternal. Amen.

**Against the Demon of Envy**

O MOST LOVING JESUS, Pattern of charity, Who makest all the commandments of the Law to consist in love towards God and towards Man, grant to us so to love Thee with all our heart, with all our mind, and all our soul, and our neighbour for Thy sake, that the grace of charity and brotherly love may dwell in us, and all envy, harshness, and ill-will may die in us; and fill our hearts with love, kindness, and compassion, so that by constantly rejoicing in the happiness and success of others, by sympathizing with them in their sorrows, and putting away all harsh judgements and envious thoughts, we may follow Thee, Who art Thyself the true and perfect love. Amen.

**Against the Demon of Sloth**

O LORD JESUS, eternal Love, Who in the garden didst pray so long and so fervently that Thy sweat was, as it were, drops of blood falling down to the ground: Put away from us, we beseech Thee, all sloth and inactivity both of body and mind; kindle within us the fire of Thy love; strengthen our weakness, that whatsoever our hand is able to do we may do earnestly, and that, striving heartily to please Thee in this life, we may have Thee hereafter as our reward exceedingly great. Amen.

## *Prayer Before a Crucifix by St. Francis of Assisi*

Most High, glorious God, enlighten the darkness of my heart. Give me, Lord, a correct faith, a certain hope, a perfect charity, sense and knowledge, so that I may carry out Your holy and true command.

## *Novena for Protection of Your House*

1 Hail Holy Queen

7 St. Michael Prayers

9 Glory Be's

3 "Lord Have Mercy On Us"

During the First World War, in France, some of the faithful Catholics were known to have this prayer tacked on their front door. These homes and residents were not harmed or invaded during the time of war. It is recommended to have in your house: holy water, blessed wax candles, and upon the doors the blessed crucifix. For the Lord will pass through striking the Egyptians; and when He shall see the blood on the transom, and on both the posts, he will pass over the door of the house, and not suffer the destroyer to come into your houses and to hurt you. [Exodus, xii] The St. Benedict Medal is among the most helpful of medals for protection. Bury one at each of the four corners of the house, and wear and keep them about. Be certain your medals are properly and fully blessed from the old Roman Ritual. Not all blessings are the same.

## *Devotion to Divine Mercy as a Means of Deliverance and Healing*

**The Chaplet of the Divine Mercy**

In 1935, Saint Faustina received a vision of an angel sent by God to chastise a certain city. She began to pray for mercy, but her prayers were powerless. Suddenly she saw the Holy Trinity and felt the power of Jesus's grace within her. At the same time, she found herself pleading with God for mercy with words she heard interiorly:

ETERNAL FATHER, I offer You the Body and Blood, Soul and Divinity of Your dearly beloved Son, Our Lord Jesus Christ, in atonement for our sins and those of the whole world. For the sake of His sorrowful Passion, have mercy on us and on the whole world (Diary, 476).

As she continued saying this inspired prayer, the angel became helpless and could not carry out the deserved punishment (see Diary, 474, 475).

The next day, as she was entering the chapel, she again heard this interior voice, instructing her how to recite the prayer that Our Lord later called "the Chaplet." From then on, she recited this form of prayer almost constantly, offering it especially for the dying.

In subsequent revelations, the Lord made it clear that the Chaplet was not just for her, but for the whole world. He also attached extraordinary promises to its recitation.

*"Encourage souls to say the Chaplet which I have given you"* (Diary, 1541).

*"Whoever will recite it will receive great mercy at the hour of death"* (Diary, 687).

*"When they say this chaplet in the presence of the dying, I will stand between My Father and the dying person, not as the just Judge but as the Merciful Saviour"* (Diary, 1541).

*"Priests will recommend it to sinners as their last hope of salvation. Even if there were a sinner most hardened, if he were to recite this chaplet only once, he would receive grace from My infinite mercy"* (Diary, 687).

*"I desire to grant unimaginable graces to those souls who trust in My mercy" (Diary, 687). "Through the Chaplet you will obtain everything, if what you ask for is compatible with My Will"* (Diary, 1731).

Prayed on ordinary rosary beads, the Chaplet of Divine Mercy is an intercessory prayer that extends the offering of the Eucharist, so it is especially appropriate to use it after having received Holy

Communion at Holy Mass. It may be said at any time, but Our Lord specifically told Saint Faustina to recite it during the nine days before the Feast of Mercy (the first Sunday after Easter). He then added: *"By this Novena, [of Chaplets] I will grant every possible grace to souls."* (Diary, 796).

It is likewise appropriate to pray the Chaplet during the "Hour of Great Mercy", three o'clock each afternoon (recalling the time of Christ's death on the Cross). In His revelations to Saint Faustina, Our Lord asked for a special remembrance of His Passion at that hour.

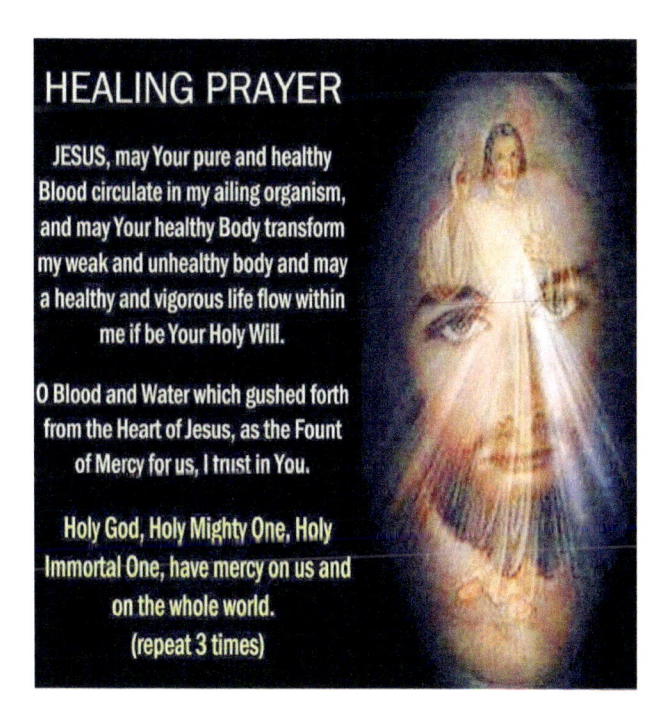

## HEALING PRAYER

JESUS, may Your pure and healthy Blood circulate in my ailing organism, and may Your healthy Body transform my weak and unhealthy body and may a healthy and vigorous life flow within me if be Your Holy Will.

O Blood and Water which gushed forth from the Heart of Jesus, as the Fount of Mercy for us, I trust in You.

Holy God, Holy Mighty One, Holy Immortal One, have mercy on us and on the whole world.
(repeat 3 times)

## The Purple Scapular of Benediction and Protection (Mystic Marie-Julie Jahenny)

The Scapular was shown in a vision on August 23, 1878 to the stigmatist and mystic Marie-Julie Jahenny (1850-1941).

The Scapular was shown to her resting on the Immaculate Heart of Mary. Marie-Julie Jahenny was born in Coyault, but lived in La Fraudais, just a short distance north of Blain in Brittany France.

<u>She was approved about three years before then by her local bishop in 1875, Bishop Fournier, Bishop of Nantes.</u> A mystic does not need approval from the Vatican; a local bishop's approval is recognised as official Church approval. Therefore, we can safely wear the Purple Scapular as it originated from a supernatural revelation given by an approved mystic.

The Scapular was specially designed by Our Lord and Our Lady Themselves, Our Lady said: *"... for a long time My Son and I have had the desire to make known this Scapular of Benediction."*

First, to remind the faithful about various details of the Passion and Our Lady's Sorrows so that they may receive their due share of veneration; and second, to protect us during the coming chastisements, for the world is already being cleansed due to its manifold sins and corruption, and it is about to get worse. Our Lady said: ***"This first apparition of this scapular will be a new protection for the times of the chastisements."***

The meaning of the symbols in Our Lady's Own words:

> "This scapular, My children, it is supposed to be made on My Heart, (i.e. with humility and devotion to Her Immaculate Heart) because **My Heart is the emblem of simplicity and humility, and hence, the colour violet.**
>
> "The nails that have pierced the Feet and the Hands of My Son have been little venerated and are venerable; hence My Son, in His Divine Wisdom, has made that these three nails be painted on the front of the scapular.
>
> "These three drops of Blood and the chalice represent the generous hearts gathering the Blood of My divine Son. (*i.e.*, those devoted to the Precious Blood and gathering it for the good of the Church, conversion of sinners, etc.)
>
> "The red sponge will represent My divine Son drinking, in a manner, the sins of His children but His Adorable Mouth refuses."

Our Lord explains the back image:

> "My children, very few souls think of wiping the Adorable Wounds of My Feet when the Blood ran, and I would like this representation to be known. They also think so little of the Tears shed by My Mother during My Passion; these Tears are found at the feet of the Angel that wipes My Sacred Feet. By this scapular,

> I would like you to think on the ladder, the reed and the nails of My Passion."

## Specific prayer or devotion that needs to be said with this Scapular?

As Our Lady presented the Scapular to Our Lord, He turned to Marie-Julie and said:

> "I address you, My victim, and also My victims and My servant, My children of the Cross, I see and I come to give you an idea and profound thought: During My descent from the Cross, they handed Me to My Mother; this descent, this thought, this devotion is little known. I would like by this reproduction on this scapular, that it pass into the hearts of the children of the Cross, <u>and that they salute Me by these three salutations</u>:

> **I salute You, Jesus Crucified, that You grant me life.**
>
> **I salute You with all the joy of the Angels and the Saints in Your descent from the Cross.**
>
> **I salute You with the sadness of Your Mother when You reposed on Her Heart and on Her Immaculate lap.**

Our Lord also asked that people meditate for at least two (2) to three(3) minutes on His Passion, and to say five(5) or seven (7) times the "Crux Ave" given to Marie-Julie Jahenny in a separate vision:

## Crux Ave #1:

**"O, CRUX AVE! Spes unica! Et Verbum caro factum est! O Jesus, Vanquisher of death, save us!"**

*(O hail to the Cross! Our only hope! And the Word was made flesh.)*

This first part must be said in Latin, and you must be "carrying" the Scapular for this prayer. Wearing it would be best!

A second 'Hail to the Cross' Prayer was also revealed to Marie-Julie Jahenny: Our Lord didn't specify which "Crux Ave" was to be said with the Scapular, so it would be a good idea to include this with the Scapular devotion as well:

## Crux Ave #2:

**I SALUTE YOU, I adore you, I embrace you, O Adorable Cross of my Saviour. Protect us, guard us, save us. Jesus loved you so much, following His example, I love you. By your holy image, calm our fears. That I feel only peace and trust!**

# MOTHER AND REFUGE

**THE PURPLE SCAPULAR WAS GIVEN TO MARIE JULIE-JAHENNY!**

## *Prayer to St. Rita for Protection*

**St. Rita of Cascia** is a **great saint of Catholic tradition**. She bore the stigmata and is responsible for many miracles: For this reason, there are many prayers dedicated to her, and for her, nothing is impossible.

## *A Prayer for Protection to the "Saint of Impossible Causes"*

O SAINT RITA, you received from the Holy Father the grace to accomplish miracles and to share your blessings with the world.

Here I am, standing before you to express my gratitude and ask for your favours.

You are called the "Saint of Impossible Causes"; keep me and my loved ones from irreparable pains, desperation, the death of the soul.

Help me obtain your many virtues: gentleness, patience, humility, love and charity towards the most vulnerable. Grant me to be pious, to have a sense of duty and an unfailing faith in the Lord.

I place myself under your protection.

Please obtain for me the Lord's forgiveness for my sins, and the strength to resist temptation.

Guide me, and guide the ones I love, through this

life on earth 'til Kingdom Come, where we will all be gathered around the table of the Heavenly Banquet. Amen.

## *POWERFUL ANCIENT PRAYER FOR DELIVERANCE*

JESUS, YOU CAME BECAUSE OF THE SICK AND THE SINFUL. Therefore, we turn to You to ask You to heal us, body and soul. You know, O Jesus, that sin harms and injures the whole human being and that it destroys relationships between mankind and You. But there is no sin and no illness that You cannot drive away with Your Almighty Word. There is no wound that You cannot heal.

Mary, You have called us to pray for healing and deliverance. We wish to do so now. We ask You to join our prayers with Yours. Pray with us now that we may be worthy of obtaining by prayer the graces we are in need of personally and for all those who are sick and infirm and in need. *(Remain in silent prayer.)*

From the Holy Gospel according to Saint Matthew:

> "At that time, Jesus got into the boat and His disciples followed Him. Without warning, a violent storm came up on the sea, and the boat began to be swamped by waves. Jesus was sleeping soundly, so they made their way toward Him and woke Him. 'Where is your courage? How little faith you have!' Then He stood up and took the winds and sea to task. Complete calm ensued; the men were dumbfounded. 'What sort of man is this,' they said, 'that even the winds and the

sea obey Him?" (Matthew 8: 23-24)

Jesus, You entered into the storms of this world. You also enter into the boat of every life. You are present, for Your Name is Emmanuel: God with us, God for us. So we are asking You now to come into our lives. The boats of our lives are also being swamped and overwhelmed. Enter, O Jesus, into the depths of our souls. We are lost. Stand and tell our unrest to be calmed; tell the waves of death that surround us to relent. Say the word to appease our hearts that they may be able to hear Your divine and creative Word. *(Remain in silent adoration.)*

Come, Jesus, into the boats of our families and of the whole world. Let our cries awaken You. Stretch out Your hand that calm may follow. Come, Lord Jesus, come. Come to where we are most wounded. *(Mention silently the areas where you know that you are wounded and need to be healed.)*

Come, Jesus, into those boats of life which stand anchored to bad habits, to drugs, to alcohol, to bodily pleasures and which cannot move forward. Jesus, calm the storms. Let all people hear Your voice which alone brings peace.

Jesus, You have called us to love. We admit that our love is weak. Heal all our wounds which have resulted from a lack of love. Cure us from all sins that prevent us from loving You above all else, O Divine Physician.

Heal in our souls all the burdens which we have accumulated throughout our childhood and youth. Vanquish all darkness and melt the ice of evil within us. Forgive our envy and jealousy, which burdens us and others. Let the grace of trust remove all mistrust and fear. Cure us of godlessness in our thoughts, in our words and in our deeds.

Jesus, heal the wounded love which we know in our families, so that it may be as it was in Yours. Heal love between spouses, between children and parents, among siblings, and among all men and women. *(Silently pray for those whom you have difficulty loving or find difficult to forgive.)*

Jesus, cleanse our souls. Enter into our minds and hearts with Your light that darkness may never overwhelm it. With the power of Your grace, touch those layers of our souls in which addictions to material things and sensual pleasures which breed fear have settled. Cleanse us that our hearts may be completely opened to You. Cure us of all inner darkness and heal the wounds in the depths of our being. Grant that we may find peace of mind and heart in You.

We ask You to free us from all mental illness and encumbrances. Lift these burdens and cleanse the wounds that develop into mental disease. Help us who have inherited heavy mental burdens. Cure us of all personality disorders, depression, fear, anxiety and every neurosis and psychopathic state. Cure us of all mental and psychological illnesses due to failures in family, in school or at work. Remove all thoughts of discouragement, despondence, suicide or forced thought.

We also ask You to forgive the sins of our ancestors whose failures have left their effects on us in the form of unwanted tendencies, behaviour patterns and defects in body, mind and spirit. Heal us, Lord, of all these disorders. Deliver us from the influence of the evil one. Free all living and deceased members of our family from every contaminating form of bondage.

Jesus, be the Master of our souls. Deliver us from all effects of occult or superstitious practices. By the power of Your Holy Name and the merits of Your Holy Cross, deliver us from every consequence of witchcraft and sorcery. Rest in every soul and restore peace to us. Amen.

## Binding Prayer

*This is a prayer used to bind demons from some kind of activity. It is recommended the commanded form of the binding prayer linked here is used only on those over which one has authority (such as a parent to child) or one's immediate family.*

SPIRIT OF N., I BIND YOU IN THE NAME OF JESUS, by the power of the most Precious Blood of Our Lord Jesus Christ and by the intercession of the Blessed Virgin Mary, St. Michael the Archangel, the blessed Apostles, Peter and Paul and all of the saints, and I command you to leave N. *(Name of person or object)* and go to the foot of the Holy Cross to receive your sentence, in the Name of the Father, the Son and the Holy Spirit. Amen.

## Prayers to Break Freemasonic Curse

*To be prayed for someone who has been involved in Freemasonry or whose ancestors have been involved in Freemasonry.* (To be prayed by one who has authority over self, spouse, parents, children).

FATHER GOD, CREATOR OF HEAVEN AND EARTH, I come to Thee in the Name of Jesus Christ Thy Son. I come as a sinner seeking forgiveness and cleansing from all sins committed against Thee, and others made in Thy image. I honour my earthly father and mother and all of my ancestors of flesh and blood, and of the spirit by adoption and godparents, but I utterly turn away from and renounce all their sins. I forgive all my ancestors for the effects of their sins on me and my children. I confess and renounce all of my own sins. I renounce and rebuke Satan and every spiritual power of his affecting me and my family. I renounce and forsake all involvement in Freemasonry or any other lodge or craft by my ancestors and myself. In the Name of Jesus Christ and by the intercession of the Blessed Virgin Mary, I renounce and cut off Witchcraft, the principal spirit behind Freemasonry, and I renounce and cut off Baphomet, the Spirit of Antichrist and the spirits of Death, and Deception. I renounce the insecurity, the love of position and power, the love of money, avarice or greed, and the pride which would have led my ancestors into Masonry. I renounce all the fears which held them in Masonry, especially the fears of death, fears of men, and fears of trusting, in the Name of Jesus Christ and by the intercession of the Blessed Virgin Mary.

I renounce every position held in the lodge by any of my ancestors or myself, including "Master," "Worshipful Master," or any other. I renounce the calling of any man "Master," for Jesus Christ is my only Lord and master, and He forbids anyone else having that title. I renounce the entrapping of others into Masonry, and observing the helplessness of others during the rituals. I renounce the effects of Masonry passed on to me through any female ancestor who may or may not have felt distrusted and rejected by her husband as he entered and attended any lodge and refused to tell her of his secret activities. I also renounce all obligations, oaths and curses enacted by every female member of my family through any direct membership of all Women's Orders of Freemasonry, the Order of the Eastern Star, or any other Masonic or occultic organization.

## *Prayer to Break Diabolic Oppression*

*This is a prayer that may be used when one suspects that there is a diabolic cause afflicting one's exterior life.*

MOST BLESSED TRINITY, by the authority given to me by the natural law and by Thy giving these things & rights to me, I claim authority, rights and power over my N. *(income, finances, possessions, etc.)* and anything else that pertains to the oppression. By the merits of Thy Sacred Wounds, I reclaim the rights, powers and authority over anything which I may have lost or conceded to any demon and I ask Thee to remove any demon's ability to influence or affect anything in my life.

God the Father, humiliate the demons that have

sought to steal Thy glory from Thee by oppressing Thy creatures. We beseech Thee to show Thy great glory and power over them and Thy great generosity to me, Thine unworthy creature, by answering all that I have asked of Thee.

I bind all demons of oppression, in the Name of Jesus, by the power of the Most Precious Blood, the power of the humility with which Christ suffered His wounds, and the intercession of the Blessed Virgin Mary, Virgin Most Powerful, Saint Michael the Archangel, the blessed Apostles, Peter and Paul, and all the saints, and I command you to leave and go to the foot of the Holy Cross to receive your sentence, in the Name of the Father, and of the Son and of the Holy Spirit. Amen.

# CONCLUSION: THE PROCESS OF DELIVERANCE: TO BE USED ONLY BY PRIESTS OR EXORCISTS

## *One: Prayer for Forgiveness*

Pray with the tormented person for the forgiveness of all sin. The person must be truly repentant and must be ready and able to forgive everyone who has harmed him/her. Ideally, have the person avail themselves of the **Sacrament of Confession** before any deliverance prayer is performed. In many cases, the demon(s) will be driven out in the Sacrament of Penance itself. In fact, confession is the "normal" method of ridding a person of demonic influence. If, after a good, exhaustive confession, the individual is still feeling harassed, proceed with the following...

## *Two: Pray the Long Version of the Exorcism Prayer of St. Michael, composed by Pope Leo XIII*

(Only priests have the authority to pray the long form. Others place themselves at risk of demonic retribution if prayed.) See Saint Michael Chapter - Six

# *Three: Pray the Litany of the Saints*

## LITANY OF THE SAINTS

*The Litany of the Saints is used in ordination, Forty Hours, processions, the Rite of Exorcism and other occasions.*

P:   LORD, HAVE MERCY.     *R. Lord, have mercy.*

P:   Christ, have mercy.     *R. Christ, have mercy.*

P:   Lord, have mercy.     *R. Lord, have mercy.*

P:   Christ, hear us.     *R. Christ, graciously hear us.*

P:   God, the Father in Heaven.     ***R. Have mercy on us.***
P: God, the Son, Redeemer of the world, *etc.*
P: God, the Holy Spirit,
P: Holy Trinity, one God,

Holy Mary,              ***R. Pray for us.***
Holy Mother of God,
Holy Virgin of virgins,
St. Michael,
St. Gabriel,

St. Raphael, **R. Pray for us.**
All holy angels and archangels, *etc.*
All holy orders of blessed spirits,
St. John the Baptist,
St. Joseph,
All holy patriarchs and prophets,
St. Peter,
St. Paul,
St. Andrew,
St. James,
St. John,
St. Thomas,
St. James,
St. Philip,
St. Bartholomew,
St. Matthew,
St. Simon,
St. Thaddeus,
St. Matthias,
St. Barnabas,
St. Luke,
St. Mark,
All holy apostles and evangelists,
All holy disciples of the Lord,
All holy Innocents,
St. Stephen,
St. Lawrence,
St. Vincent,
SS. Fabian and Sebastian,
SS. John and Paul,

SS. Cosmas and Damian,
SS. Gervase and Protase,
All holy martyrs,
St. Sylvester,          **R. Pray for us.**
St. Gregory, *etc.*
St. Ambrose,
St. Augustine,
St. Jerome,
St. Martin,
St. Nicholas,
All holy bishops and confessors,
All holy doctors,
St. Anthony,
St. Benedict,
St. Bernard,
St. Dominic,
St. Francis,
All holy priests and levites,
All holy monks and hermits,
St. Mary Magdalen,
St. Agatha,
St. Lucy,
St. Agnes,
St. Cecilia,
St. Catherine,
St. Anastasia,
All holy virgins and widows,

P: All holy saints of God,      R. *Intercede for us.*

P: Be merciful,     R. *Spare us, O Lord.*

P:  Be merciful,         R. *Graciously hear us, O Lord.*

From all evil,         **R. *Deliver us, O Lord.***
From all sin, *etc.*
From Your wrath,
From sudden and unprovided death,   **R. *Deliver us, O Lord.***
From the snares of the devil, *etc.*
From anger, hatred, and all ill will,
From all lewdness,
From lightning and tempest,
From the scourge of earthquakes,
From plague, famine, and war,
From everlasting death,
By the mystery of your holy Incarnation,
By Your coming,
By Your Birth,
By Your Baptism and holy fasting,
By Your Cross and Passion,
By Your Death and Burial,
By Your holy Resurrection,
By Your wondrous Ascension,
By the coming of the Holy Spirit, the Advocate,
On the Day of Judgment,

P:  We sinners,       **R. *We beg You to hear us.***
That You spare us, *etc.*
That You pardon us,
That You bring us to true penance,
That You govern and preserve Your holy Church,
That You preserve our Holy Father,

and all ranks in the Church in holy religion,
That You humble the enemies of holy Church,
That You give peace and true concord to all Christian rulers,
That You give peace and unity to the whole Christian world,
That You restore to the unity of the Church all who have strayed from the truth, and lead all unbelievers to the light of the
Gospel,
That You confirm and preserve us in Your holy service,
That You lift up our minds to heavenly desires,
**R. *We beg You to hear us.***
That You grant everlasting blessings to all our benefactors, *etc.*
That You deliver our souls and the souls of our brethren, relatives, and benefactors from everlasting damnation,
That You give and preserve the fruits of the earth,
That You grant eternal rest to all the faithful departed,
That You graciously hear us,
Son of God,

*At the end of the litany, he (the priest) adds the following:*

P: Antiphon: Do not keep in mind, O Lord, our offenses or those of our parents, nor take

vengeance on our sins.
P: Our Father…

## Four: Renunciation

Have the tormented person *renounce* each area of bondage and *bind* the wicked, demonic spirits, all in the Name of Jesus. For example, you might use the following words: *"In the Name of Jesus, I renounce and bind the spirits of lust. In the Name of Jesus, I renounce and bind the spirits of pride, etc."* It is important that the individual first identify the areas of bondage and that he or she personally renounce these spirits. You, as the deliverance minister, can lead the person in the renunciation process, especially if the person is timid, shy, or just uncomfortable. (Only exorcists can do this usually, as they are given a special charism/authority that protects them as per the advice of Fr. Ripperger.)

To be sure that you have renounced all possible areas of bondage, below is a fairly comprehensive list of common areas of bondage to be renounced, should they apply. A good rule-of-thumb is to renounce and bind every one of the possible areas of bondage listed, so as to err on the side of caution:

> "Envy, criticism, impatience, resentment, pride, rebellion, stubbornness, unforgiveness, gossip, disobedience, strife, violence, divorce, accusation,

anger, manipulation, jealousy, greed, laziness, revenge, coveting, possessiveness, control, retaliation, selfishness, deceitfulness, deception, dishonesty, unbelief, seduction, lust, pornography, masturbation, idolatry, witchcraft, physical and psychological infirmities, nerve disorder, lung disorder, brain disorder or dysfunction, AIDS, cancer, hypochondriasis, hyperactivity, depression, schizophrenia, fatigue, anorexia, bulimia, addictions, gluttony, perfectionism, alcoholism, self-abuse, sexual addictions, sexual perversions, attempted suicide, incest, pedophilia, lesbianism, homosexuality, adultery, homophobia, confusion, ignorance, procrastination, self-hatred, isolation, loneliness, ostracism, paranoia, nervousness, passivity, indecision, doubt, oppression, rejection, poor self-image, anxiety, shame, timidity, fear, and finally, each of the seven deadly sins and everything that leads to a failure to love God with all of one's heart, soul, strength and mind, and a everything that leads to a failure to love one's brothers and sisters as Christ has loved us."

Be sure not to forget to have the individual renounce any authority over his/her life that he/she might have given inadvertently to a soothsayer, a psychic, fortune-teller, etc, by stating, *"In the Name of Jesus, I renounce the authority over my life I gave to (name of fortune-teller), and to the spirit that operated in (name)."* Bondage can additionally be the result of sexual unions the person has had outside of the context of marriage. Such bondage is referred to as a soul-tie. In this instance, have the person say, *"In the Name of Jesus, I renounce all sexual and spiritual bondage to (name of person), and I take back the authority I gave to him/her."*

## Five: Take Authority (Only for Priests and Exorcists)

This is where spiritual confrontation and combat occur. Pray over the afflicted person (Only for priests and exorcists) using the following formula: "In the Name of Jesus I break and dissolve the power of every spirit that *(name)* has renounced and any related spirit, and I command them now to leave in the Name of Jesus, to depart quietly, without manifestation or harm to anyone, and I command you to go straight to Jesus, and to the foot of His Cross, for Him to deal with you as He sees fit." You, as a deliverance minister, may want to have the afflicted person speak the words of command for him or herself. Either way, this is the crux of the deliverance.

## Six: Pray the Litany of Holy Command:

The Litany of Holy Command, a deliverance prayer, was given in recent years by Archangel Michael, for use by any of the faithful in a state of grace (Nwoye, B. 2009. *The breeze of the Second Pentecost*). Following are St. Michael's words regarding the

## Litany and the prayer itself:

> "I come to give you the 'Litany of Holy Command,' which you have as a Catholic, but many of you do not know . . . Mortal man, you have the Holy Mass, the greatest prayer on Earth. You have your Rosary, the Chaplet of the Precious Blood, and all the devotional prayers of the Church. These are the great prayers that have power over the hosts of demons. With these prayers, your authorities as a child of God, and this 'Litany of Holy Command,' a mortified child of God will drive away any type of demon from whatever level" (Archangel Michael).

> (Only over those you have authority... *i.e.,* spouses, parents and children)

### The Litany of Holy Command

I COMMAND YOU, whoever you may be, unclean spirits, wicked spirits of Hell, to give place to the Holy Spirit of God, Who owns this/these Temple(s).

*Deliver us (him/her), O Lord, by the Power of Your Holy Name.*

In the Name and by the Power of the True God, the Holy God, and the Only Living God,

*Deliver us (him/her), O Lord, by the Power of Your Holy Name.*

I command you, in the Name of Our Lord Jesus Christ to leave this/these Temple(s) and return to the abyss.

*Deliver us (him/her), O Lord, by the Power of Your Holy Name.*

In the Name of the Precious Blood of the Spotless Lamb of God, I command you.

*Deliver us (him/her), O Lord, by the Power of Your Holy Name.*

In the Name of the Holy Ghost, I command you.

*Deliver us (him/her), O Lord, by the Power of Your Holy Name.*

In the Name of Holy Mary, who crushed your head, I command you.

*Deliver us (him/her), O Lord, by the Power of Your Holy Name.*

Her Immaculate Conception commands you.

*Deliver us (him/her), O Lord, by the Power of Your Holy Name.*

Her Virginity and Purity command you.

*Deliver us (him/her), O Lord, by the Power of Your Holy Name.*

Her holy Obedience, Patience, and Humility command you.

*Deliver us (him/her), O Lord, by the Power of Your Holy Name.*

Her Heart, pierced with the swords of Sorrows, commands you.

*Deliver us (him/her), O Lord, by the Power of Your Holy Name.*

Her glorious Assumption commands you.

*Deliver us (him/her), O Lord, by the Power of Your Holy Name.*

Depart! You infernal spirits, in the Name of Mary; Queen of Heaven and earth.

*Deliver us (him/her), O Lord, by the Power of Your Holy Name.*

In the Name of the Holy, Catholic, and Apostolic Church, I command you.

*Deliver us (him/her), O Lord, by the Power of Your Holy Name.*

The faith of Peter and Paul and of all the Apostles commands you.

*Deliver us (him/her), O Lord, by the Power of Your Holy Name.*

The blood of Martyrs commands you.

*Deliver us (him/her), O Lord, by the Power of Your Holy Name.*

The purity of Virgins and of all the Saints commands you.

*Deliver us (him/her), O Lord, by the Power of Your Holy Name.*

Be gone, you wicked legions, in the Name of the Holy Catholic Faith.

*Deliver us (him/her), O Lord, by the Power of Your*

*Holy Name.*

In the Name and by the Power of the Eucharistic Jesus Christ present in the Tabernacles all over the world, I command you.

*Deliver us (him/her), O Lord, by the Power of Your Holy Name.*

The Sacred Chalice, which contains the Precious Blood of Jesus Christ commands you.

*Deliver us (him/her), O Lord, by the Power of Your Holy Name.*

The Sacred Sign of the Cross commands you.

*Deliver us (him/her), O Lord, by the Power of Your Holy Name.*

Flee, you disobedient, by the merits of the Holy Wounds of Our Lord Jesus Christ.

*Deliver us (him/her), O Lord, by the Power of Your Holy Name.*

In the Name of God, the Father Almighty, and by the obedience of His Angels, I command you.

*Deliver us (him/her), O Lord, by the Power of Your Holy Name.*

The Celestial Choirs of Seraphim and Cherubim command you.

*Deliver us (him/her), O Lord, by the Power of Your Holy Name.*

The Celestial Choirs of Thrones and Dominions command you.

*Deliver us (him/her), O Lord, by the Power of Your Holy Name.*

The Celestial Choirs of Powers and Virtues command you.

*Deliver us (him/her), O Lord, by the Power of Your Holy Name.*

The Celestial Choir of Principalities commands you.

*Deliver us (him/her), O Lord, by the Power of Your Holy Name.*

The Celestial Choir of Angels commands you.

*Deliver us (him/her), O Lord, by the Power of Your Holy Name.*

The Celestial Choir of Archangels commands you.

*Deliver us (him/her), O Lord, by the Power of Your Holy Name.*

O God of Heaven and earth, God of Angels and Archangels, Who is like Thee? I beg You to rebuke these wicked spirits by the Power of Your Holy Name.

*Deliver us (him/her), O Lord, by the Power of Your Holy Name.*

Jesus, the Son of the ever-Virgin, I adore Your Blood of Circumcision and beseech You to deliver us by

Your Precious Blood.

*Deliver us by Your Precious Blood.*

Jesus, the only begotten Son of God, by Your Sweat of Blood,

*Deliver us by Your Precious Blood.*

Jesus, the Sacrificial Lamb, by Your Scourging,

*Deliver us by Your Precious Blood.*

Jesus, crowned with Thorns,

*Deliver us by Your Precious Blood.*

Jesus, Who carried the Cross for our Salvation,

*Deliver us by Your Precious Blood.*

Jesus Crucified,

*Deliver us by Your Precious Blood.*

Jesus, pierced on the Side from which Blood and Water come out,

*Deliver us by Your Precious Blood.*

Jesus, I beseech You to save us. Amen.

Let us pray.

O God, set Your children free who are possessed by the powers of darkness + In the Name of the Father + and of the Son + and of the Holy Spirit. Amen.

## Seven: Prayer of Thanksgiving

*Once the person has been set free, pray in thanksgiving to Jesus:*

THANK YOU, JESUS, for setting (name) free. Thank you, Jesus, for releasing him/her from the bondage to (name area of bondage). Amen.

## Eight: Prayer of Blessing

*Pray that the newly freed individual might be blessed anew in the Holy Spirit. You might use the following words:*

COME, HOLY SPIRIT. Come by the means of the most powerful intercession of the Immaculate Heart of Mary, Your well-beloved Spouse, and fill this person with your many gifts and blessings. Please fill up any areas that have been left vacant by the departure of evil spirits. Fill any and all vacancies with the love, the joy, the peace, healing and light of the Risen Lord Jesus Christ. We now ask You to bless and seal *(name)* in the Blood of Jesus Christ, the price of our salvation. Amen.

## Nine: Re-dedication and Re-consecration

*Re-dedicate this living temple to the Divine Will of God*

*the Father, to the Precious Blood of Jesus, and to the Sacred Hearts of Jesus and Mary. The following prayer of consecration is most effective in the re-dedication and re-consecration of the Lord's Living Temple to Jesus through Mary:*

## *Act of Consecration to the Sacred Heart of Jesus through the Immaculate Heart of Mary in the Spirit of St. Joseph*

HAIL, HOLY QUEEN OF HEAVEN AND EARTH, Refuge of Sinners, Woman clothed with the Sun (cf. Rev 12:1), Virgin of Fatima, Spouse of the Holy Spirit, our Spiritual Mother (cf. Jn 19:26) and Mediatrix of all Grace and Mercy; we, the Apostles of Light of Your Immaculate Heart, come before You this day to renew, through, with and in Your Immaculate Heart, the solemn vows made at our Baptism. We firmly reject Satan, the ancient serpent (cf. Rev 12:9), the father of lies, and a murderer from the beginning (cf. Jn 8:44), whose head, swollen with pride, shall be crushed beneath Your heel (cf. Gen 3:15), and of whose poison cup we refuse to drink; we reject this world and its vanities, of which the devil is prince (cf. Jn 12:31); finally, we reject every form of impurity of mind, body and spirit.

In the presence of the most high Triune God and His cloud of heavenly witnesses (cf. Heb 12:1-2), the angels and saints, we take You, O Blessed Virgin Mary, as our Spiritual Mother (cf. Jn 19:26); and we hereby espouse Your Immaculate Heart (cf. Sir 15:1-2), that, in imitation of St. Joseph and under his fatherly protection, our hearts might beat in a perfect union of love with and for the most Sacred and Eucharistic Heart of Jesus, the Christ, for all time and eternity. Moreover, through our mutual exchange of hearts, O sweetest Queen Mother, may the Triumph of Your Immaculate Heart take place in our souls.

Furthermore, O gracious Virgin, we pray that You might nourish our parched souls with the milk of divine grace. May our hearts, like Yours, blossom into lush gardens of heavenly delights, virtues and graces, and become fitting temples for Your divine Spouse, the most Holy Spirit of God (cf. 1 Cor 3:16), thereby grafting and uniting us ever more perfectly to the Mystical Body of Christ (cf. 1 Cor 12:12) and reproducing in our souls the image of Christ crucified.

Thus, we solemnly entrust and consecrate to You, O Immaculate Virgin Mary, in our abject misery, poverty, weakness, sinfulness and nothingness, everything that we are and have, just as we are, without reserve: body, soul, intellect, will and emotions; all of our interior and exterior goods and possessions; and even the satisfactory, meritorious value of all our good works – past, present and future – for You to dispose of according to the designs of Your Immaculate Heart, in anticipation of the promised Triumph of Your Immaculate Heart in the Church and the world and the long-awaited establishment of the holy city, the new Jerusalem, that shall come down out of Heaven, and in which Christ shall establish His glorious Eucharistic reign of peace, justice, holiness and love (cf. Rev 21:2).

Like a lamb led to the slaughter who opens not his mouth (cf. Acts 8:32), we place ourselves and the spiritual sacrifices of our prayers, works and especially the sufferings of this day and of our entire lives on the consecrated altar of Your Immaculate Heart. Please unite each one of us and our offerings to Jesus's spotless and unblemished offering of Himself to the perfect glorification of the Eternal Father, renewed this day and every day, from the rising of the sun to its setting, in the Most Holy Sacrifice of the Mass. We make this offering in atonement for the sins of our whole lives and for those of the whole world, in a profound act of glorification, adoration, gratitude, expiation and supplication to the Most Holy Trinity, for the intentions of the Two Sacred Hearts of Jesus and Mary, for the Church's solemn recognition and definition of Your Spiritual Motherhood, Mary, as the "Co-redemptrix, Mediatrix and Advocate," and for the conversion, sanctification and salvation of all souls until the end of time.

In imitation of Christ, Your dearly beloved Son, "the Firstborn of all creation" (cf. Col 1:15), we humbly request that the chalice of suffering might be taken from us (cf. Lk 22:42); yet, with Christ and in imitation of You, O Holy Virgin, we ultimately submit our unconditional and irrevocable *fiat* to the Divine Will of the Eternal Father as we state, "Behold the servant of the Lord; be it done to me according to Thy Word" (cf. Lk 1:38); and we patiently accept, in advance, whatever crosses and sufferings that the Divine Heart of God the Father chooses to send us (cf. Lk 1:38). O Mother and Mediatrix of all Grace and Mercy, may we truly participate in Your fullness of Grace and be clothed with Your own heroic faith, hope, charity, purity, humility, fortitude, and that perfect resignation of will necessary to deny our very selves, pick up our crosses daily, and follow Jesus (cf. Lk 9:23) on the narrow path of evangelical poverty, chastity and obedience; bearing witness to our faith in Christ and His Holy Gospel in all of our thoughts, words and deeds, even to the point of the shedding of our blood, should we be called to wear the holy crown of martyrdom.

And when our mission on this earth has been accomplished, we pray that, as the littlest of Your many children and the smallest flowers in the Garden of Your Immaculate Heart, You Mary, along with Your Divine Son Jesus, might be present at our side with Your glorified bodies to receive our dying breath and to escort our souls straight to the Throne of the Thrice Holy Godhead; that the Eternal Father, seeing reproduced in our souls the image of His crucified Christ, might invite us to the Eternal Banquet, the heavenly wedding feast of the Lamb and His Bride, the Church (cf. Rev 19:9). Furthermore, having comprised the humble "heel" of the Mystical Body used by You, Mary, to crush the head of the ancient serpent (cf. Gen: 3:15), may we, one day, make up bright, shining stars in the crown about Your Most Immaculate Heart (cf. Rev 12:1). And may we behold He Who is, Who was, and Who shall be for all eternity, participating in the merits of the angels and saints in paradise and in the eternal chorus of praise, glory, wisdom, thanks, honour, power and might to our God forever and forever (cf. Rev 7:12). Amen.

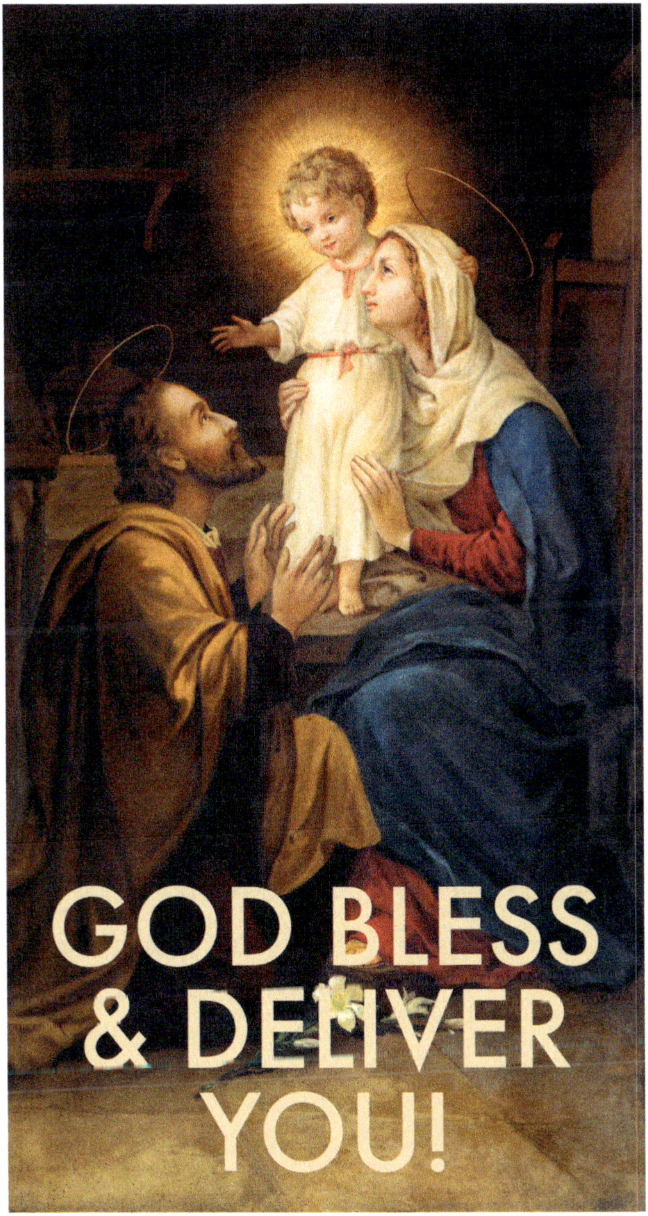
GOD BLESS
& DELIVER
YOU!

## Ten: Protection of the Deliverance Minister

**(Not for the laity)**

After the deliverance has taken place, the deliverance minister should offer some prayers to be protected against any spirits seeking revenge on him or her for doing the Lord's work. The devil will be angry that you have released a soul from his captivity and may desire to attack the deliverance minister. To avoid this, claim the Precious, shed Blood of Jesus over all aspects of your life, ministry, airspace, sources of supply, your physical, psychological, and spiritual health and wellbeing. Further, ask the Blessed Mother to intercede for both you and the one who has just been delivered, that She might shield you both from the snares and the attacks of the enemy by enfolding you and the one Jesus delivered through you in Her Immaculate Heart and covering you with Her Immaculate mantle of protection, holiness and purity.

Adapted from Marian Apostolate Website

# ACKNOWLEDGEMENT

We would like to acknowledge the following sources in which some of the content from this book was adapted:

https://www.catholicexorcism.org/deliverance-prayers-for-the-laity
https://whitelilyoftrinity.com/aspirations.html
https://catholicgentleman.com
https://romancatholicman.com/wp/st-benedict-medal-with-exorcism-blessing/
https://www.catholiccompany.com/content/prayers-st-benedict-of-nursia#
https://www.guerisonetdelivrance.com/en/pages/prayers/prayers-of-deliverance/page-8.html
https://www.churchpop.com/2016/07/07/demons-in-the-desert-the-epic-spiritual-warfare-of-st-anthony-the-great/
https://www.familyofsaintsharbel.org/prayers.html
https://www.discerninghearts.com/catholic-podcasts/st-charbel-prayers-chaplet-and-devotions/
https://catholicexchange.com/spiritual-warfare-lessons-from-st-padre-pio/

https://hozana.org/en/prayer/padre-pio/protection
https://www.prayer-warrior.com/prayers-by-enoch
https://www.ewtn.com/catholicism/devotions/chaplet-of-st-michael-the-archangel-386https://mysaintmyhero.com/blogs/my-saint-my-hero-blog/why-you-should-always-wear-the-miraculous-medal
https://blog.cancaonova.com/catholicismanew/2017/02/01/prayer-of-deliverance-the-most-precious-blood-of-jesus/
http://marian.org/divinemercy/prayers.html
https://marianapostolate.com/deliverance/

# ABOUT THE AUTHOR

## Mother And Refuge Of The End Times

Mother and Refuge of the End Times is made up of a group of lay and clerical volunteers who share the mission of spreading the messages of Heaven to the world. Our ministry consists of YouTube Channels, prayer groups on Telegram and other social media sites and a website. We hope that this prayerbook will be spiritually enriching and a source of hope and deliverance to you and your family. May God bless you and keep you!

Find us at: www.motherandrefuge.com

# BOOKS BY THIS AUTHOR

## Pieta Of The Apocalypse: Essential End Time Prayers And Promises

We are well aware of the lateness of the hour, and we would like to equip you for this time of tribulation, with this little book of treasures from heaven.

The prayers in this book have been given to Catholic end time seers and mystics over the last century or more. Our Lord Jesus and his Blessed Mother Mary have warned us of the apocalyptic times that we are now facing. They have also blessed us with an abundance of grace filled devotions to assist us through this valley of tears.

Therefore, all the prayers in this book have been directly given to us by heaven for our help and assistance in these end times.

We pray that this book of prayers may be with its

faithful owner throughout these difficult times and be a tool to aid the reader in lifting his or her soul up to heaven and reaching his or her soul's desired end which is intimate unity with Christ, Our Lord.

We ask the Lord that this book of end time prayers be for you a means of reaching the spiritual refuge of the Immaculate Heart of Mary and Sacred Heart of Jesus.

As we behold the body of Our Lord Jesus in the arms of his loving Mother, in the Pieta, today, we also reflect upon the lifeless body of Christ, the Church, in the arms of our Blessed Mother Mary. Our Lady holds the church close to her Immaculate Heart as it journeys through its own way of the cross. In the arms of Our Lady, we too hold firm hope that the Church, The Mystical Body of Christ, will soon experience its rebirth and resurrection like its Master. As the Church experiences its painful and sorrowful Calvary, we close to the Our Blessed Mother, are eagerly awaiting a promised Era of Peace and the triumph of the Eucharistic Jesus in a united and renewed Church that imitates the Lord in all things.

Printed in Great Britain
by Amazon